# Have A Nice Day!

~ Easier Said Than Done ~

Shawn Sandt

ISBN 978-1-957077-92-5

Publishing assistance by BookCrafters, Parker, Colorado.
www.bookcrafters.net

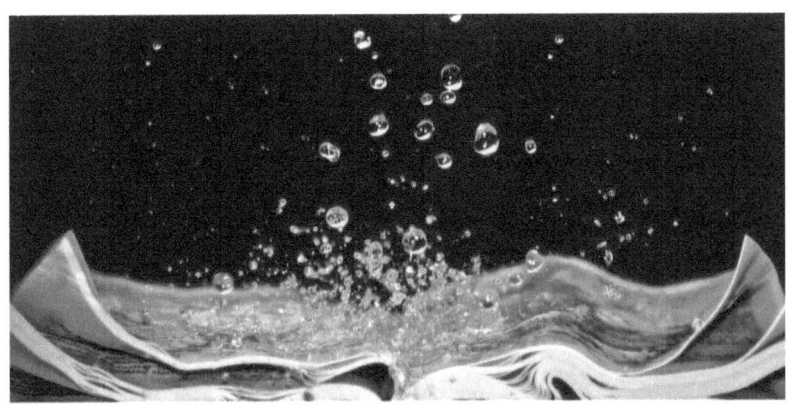

# Thirst for Knowledge

The rules.....

First, in sports betting, you may hear the term over/under. When you take the combined number of points between two teams within a particular game, you can bet either the over or the under of that total. Every single game is different. In any game, even say Super Bowl 48 perhaps, the game had the over/under set at 47 a week before the game, but on the day of the big game, it moved to 48. Most of the betting public (gamblers) was going on the over and Vegas, the group that sets the odds and drives the "action," (a fancy word for "bet"), was all going on the over. Most that were betting on the game were predicting the game would score a combined amount greater than 47. So much so, the odds makers who set and control the line (most often by guys in Vegas) move it a little to balance the "action" or the wagering. The line ended at kickoff on 48 for the Super Bowl. The entire world thought the game would go OVER.

The story you are about to read is about 88% true and accurate. I'd lean heavier on the over. I have changed almost every single name in this book for the protection of everyone included, especially myself. That's not true, but I should have changed my name in real life years ago, it would have made hiding easier to pull off. Please don't judge me, but for a short time, I was a real dumbass.

I'll also apologize in advance to my mother for the bad words that she'll run across while reading this. Sorry, Mom. As much as I'll try to keep this book PG-13, for accuracy reasons, a good ole' F-bomb will be required here and there.

I hope you, the reader, enjoy the story you are about to read.

I also hope if you or anyone else you know is in a bad spot for doing something stupid there is always a way out. I hope you find wisdom through the story and inspiration within this book to be a better person. That's all I ever wanted.

As I tell this story these days to friends, family, and even a stranger here and there, we all have some good laughs. Back then, I didn't tell anyone, and it wasn't so funny. I'm not sure why, but there is an odd comfort now having survived an ordeal like this. Without a doubt, these were the toughest four years of my life.

# 1

# Ravens

*"If you lose self-control, everything will fall."*
—John Wooden

THIRD DOWN AND FOUR YARDS TO GO from their own 30-yard line. The Ravens were facing a running clock and were down by 7. The time left on the clock was slowly ticking away. 39, 38, 37, they had no timeouts, and the clock continued to tick away. The QB (remember I'm not using real names, or names at all if possible) was trying to hurry his team along. The Baltimore Ravens were playing the Broncos in Denver in the divisional round of the playoffs in January of 2013. Denver had covered the spread and the game's point total was 63. I was good on my parlay bet; (we'll go over what a parlay is soon) I just needed this game to be over.

36, 35, the clock continued to count down as the Ravens QB snapped the ball on third down only needing a little completion to move the chains and get a first down. Although the Ravens had no time-outs, they could possibly maneuver the ball using the sidelines and quick passes to move closer to the end zone. The clock was not on their side, and it was starting to become a big problem. Not for me though, "please end this damn game," was all I was thinking. I at one point screamed at the TV, "Run clock, run!!!"

The Ravens were down by a touchdown and the end zone was 70 yards away. Once the ball snapped, the pocket collapsed around him. Denver's defense was bringing heat. This play was almost, rather, should have been over before the pass was even attempted. Oddly the QB wound up his throwing arm and released a sort of Hail Mary.

"Right now?" I thought. "This is perfect!" I uttered to myself as the play was unfolding.

A Hail Mary is usually the last desperate attempt once you get into a position a little better than your own 30-yard line. As the TV camera tracked the ball in mid-air, I had a slight excitement come over me. What kind of idiot tosses this kind of pass with 30 seconds or so on the clock on third down? The history of a Hail Mary scoring a touchdown in football games might be like .02% success. That's when it's tossed from midfield or better. Having been thrown from their own 30-yard line? I've never seen it done, EVER!

The cornerback for the Broncos who was covering the wide receiver was probably as shocked at the play call as the rest of the world. He was so far from the receiver that the announcers on TV calling the game mentioned that he was probably in another coverage scheme. Ya think? "He had coverage help over the top from the safety." That was kind of the announcers to mention that and let him off the hook. Having watched the replay in disbelief no less than 100 times, it was complete BS.

Well, the safety, (I'll keep the name withheld but he did have a cute little nickname, "The Dream,") he played the ball equally badly. Yup, first the cornerback, and now the safety. The Greek tragedy was unfolding live for the entire world to see. This wasn't any kind of dream though, what was unfolding was nothing short of a nightmare.

"The Dream" jumped up to deflect the ball away from the receiver just a tad early. Like really early. Before the football was in the same zip code, and as you can guess, he completely missed it. "What the hell was that?" is all I could think in disbelief. "Please God, let the receiver drop the ball," is all I remember thinking.

At this point I was riding an emotional roller coaster. Just a mere second or two prior I was giggling inside and all giddy, and now watching a Hail Mary? Then the floor dropped in my stomach and the smile dissolved off my face. What in the world is going on? The excitement watching this play unfold quickly eroded at the tail end of this disaster. The receiver caught the ball and two seconds later, he jogged into the end zone. He was never touched. He didn't spike the ball, do any silly touchdown dance, nothing. He was as shocked as anyone at what had just gone down. The game was tied at 35 and it was going into overtime.

Right now, I was in trouble winning my bet. The over/under for the game total was a lock. That wasn't a problem, I couldn't lose there. We were at 70, and someone had to at least kick a field goal to win this game. My problem was the spread. Denver was predicted to win this by at least 4 points. I had them covering, and winning by a field goal wouldn't help. That would only be 3, and they wouldn't be covering the 4.

Field goals are the deciding factor in most overtime football games. Like 97% of the time. I'd lose my two-game parlay if Denver couldn't score a touchdown in overtime. Perhaps an interception returned for a touchdown? Maybe a kickoff returned all the way for a score? Just a few short years earlier, we had a Heisman-winning QB throw a pass in overtime against the Steelers to win a playoff game. Could we do it again? I was hard at it creating the win in my head, like I myself could will it to happen.

The correct way to reference this kind of bet is called a two-team parlay. Pick two games or two different bets within the same game and you have a parlay. I had bet $800 on this game today making a two-team parlay. Denver to cover the spread of 4, and the point total for the game, an over. The truth, at this point in the game, tied at 35, I knew I probably wasn't going to win. I had to win both bets to win the total bet. Denver had to score a TD in overtime for me to win the parlay bet. Wining it would pay almost $2,000. The payout for hitting only one part of the bet? Well, that would be zero!

Of course, being a Broncos fan, I wanted the Broncos to continue winning football games. Plus having their new legendary quarterback reach another Super Bowl is always what most football fans wanted. Broncos fans or not, it's good for the game. The Broncos were the best team in the NFL that year and winning another Lombardy Trophy was just a couple weeks away. Only one problem that day, the Ravens ended the game in double overtime with a field goal.

**********

I'd been in this hole too many times over the past couple years. Far too many times for comfort. This is about the time in my life I a ran across a great one-liner, "The definition of insanity is doing the same thing over and over again expecting a different result." Words that would have better served me if I acted on them 10 years ago, perhaps.

When you gamble on sports, especially on football, you'll spend the better part of the week preparing for the hell of kickoff. Oddly, game day is something that you'll not look forward to. Like going to the dentist perhaps. You'll like the prospect of having that cavity filled and the pain gone, but the process during and ultimately the bill you'll face at the end of the visit is far from any kind of pleasure.

Bluntly, it sucks, and every single game changes how you watch it. That is, if you have a bet on it. I've not bet on the Broncos on a particular weekend and had my entire paycheck riding on say Cleveland playing Miami. I might not even watch the Broncos game if it was being played at the same time as the game(s) I had money on.

About midway through your Sunday, you'll be up or down going into the Sunday night game. Sometimes you're playing on house money, but too often you'll be chasing money already lost earlier in the day. There is nothing worse than watching the late game Sunday night with two teams playing that you have no direct interest in, all because you are hoping the teams score 51 points so you can go to bed a winner. It's beyond painful waiting for a final kick or some other nonsense to happen to see if your bet comes through. Of course, when you're down and desperate needing a win, you know that kick is going to be missed with 3 seconds left and the point total ended at 49. Ughh.... another loss! Try enjoying the rest of your evening.

Every week, all that drama of football and your preparation normally starts on Thursday. Which teams am I going to bet on this week? It's a sickness for sure, some call it a disease. About the same time Thursday morning, the NFL releases the weekly injury report. The NFL requires each team to post any and all injuries for their team that week. Without exception, every team, every single week. Say what you want, that report is required due to its impact on gambling. If the star quarterback is "iffy" on playing due to perhaps an ankle injury, the point total or line could shift several points in a certain direction if he plays or not.

After you read the injury report, you'll start looking into matchups. If team A is a dominating passing team, and their opponent, team B has a horrible defense that might suggest team A will score a lot of points. Well, right there might be an "over" bet or a "cover" bet opportunity. Unless of course that same team, team A, is playing against the current sack leader in the NFL on Team B, perhaps your QB won't get to score much because he'll be running for his life all night. Then don't forget to check the weather forecast.... Throwing long balls in the bitter cold of Cleveland never works well for high scoring games. Or does it? After all, you have the defending Super Bowl champs in town. Then you might read about team A's history against team B's. Is there a past perhaps? Maybe coach A got fired from team B three years ago and hates them with a passion? In Denver we had a Superbowl-winning coach who was fired as the head coach a few years prior by the Raiders, a division rival; and when we played them, almost like clockwork, Denver rarely lost those games. Although his team is playing badly this year, that coach never loses to Team B. All this research is normally done before lunch on Thursday. I'd normally spend the next couple of days verifying little details and talking with others about my picks. Are you following me on the madness?

During football season, my typical action was spent on NFL games. I would also play the college games on Friday nights and all-day Saturdays, but far too often all I would do is bury myself in debt before the NFL games even started on Sunday. Seemed like week in and week out, I was always playing catch-up. The games, spreads, and lack of information on the college game just didn't fit me to be any good at it. Betting college games that is. I'd of course come to that conclusion far too late. Week in and week out, I spent the bulk of my study time on the NFL schedule.

The Broncos having lost that game cost me a true $800. Honestly, I was bothered more at having lost the opportunity of winning $2,000. In a reckless behavior, I thought the best way to avenge that loss was with a couple easy bets on the AFC and NFC championship games the next weekend. Then of course, I could wrap up the season with a nice win by betting a good-sized amount on the Super Bowl. All I had to do was bet against the Ravens. Having just beat the Broncos, they were my new favorite team to hate.

They didn't deserve or earn the right to be playing past the Broncos game. Obviously, that was just my opinion. I didn't care who they were playing in the Championship game. I was going heavy against them. As it turns out, they won the AFC Championship game and were now off to the Super Bowl. Betting against them on championship weekend to maybe win some money hadn't worked well either.

Going into Super Bowl Sunday, I had zero doubt the Ravens would lose. I was in the hole on my post-season betting. Their BS win in Denver and then the road game win in the AFC Championship the following weekend really buried me financially. I had only one chance to get back to even. Heck, perhaps maybe I could even add a few dollars to my wallet. All I had to do was hit the Super Bowl correctly.

If you follow football, you probably know how that went. Not just for the Ravens but for my money issue. I wasn't just in the hole but buried alive and in some deep trouble. Little did I know how bad or rather how deep that hole was, but I was going to find out real soon.

# 2

# March 2013

*"Do not judge, so that you will not be judged, since you will be judged in the same judgment that you make, and you will be measured by the same standard you apply."*
—Matthew 7:1–2

A GOOD FRIEND OF MINE called me one day in March a little over two months after my Super Bowl meltdown. I'd lost a chunk of money betting on the Broncos that year, and I went out with a bang betting against the Ravens in the Super Bowl. Far from a good bang unfortunately. I bet every dime I had plus some against the Ravens. You probably watched that game somewhere and can imagine how that turned out for me. Anyway, my friend and I spoke a few times a week, more so during football season. However, it was one day he called with a slightly different agenda. Let's call him Bart.

Why Bart, you ask? Well, I've only known two Barts in my life. One was a childhood pal that I grew up with. That kid was a good athlete, a marginal student, and always had this funny look on his face that guaranteed nobody would ever take him seriously. In or out of school, you almost always knew he was always up to something. He was the most loveable guy, but to say he was off a tad, well that would be an understatement. If Bart wasn't currently in trouble for something, it was only a matter of time. The other Bart I knew of was Bart Simpson. That's right, the famous cartoon character. My real friend Bart was Bart long before the Simpson version ever got famous.

Anyway, Bart "the guy in this story" who had called me was one of my better friends and he was the one that introduced me to sports betting. Even though I had made little wagers on football games in casinos and various side bets with friends or perhaps co-workers in the past, I knew what I was doing. Bart introduced me to the many kinds of sports bets. Many don't know, but there's more than just a straight up bet. He also introduced me to what "Vig" or "Lay" means? He covered and went over everything with me. Bart would even pace me (monitor my bets and keep me out of trouble) throughout the season. He explained strategy and odds that many gamblers don't ever consider or understand. There's a ton of math to it and a hell of a lot more science than most would ever understand. We went over odds week in and week out like we were in a lifetime college class. Bart was also the man who introduced me to my first bookie. We called him JB.

Back to that call in March. "What in the hell are you doing?" Bart asked jokingly, but his intentions were good with the direct question.

My new bookie JB was also booking all of Bart's action. Bart and JB knew each other well, really well actually. Bart had bet with him for years prior to me being introduced. Bart and JB had worked together for some time. That's right, worked together.

After several years betting with JB, Bart started introducing other players (guys like me) to JB. Bart was now an affiliate for JB. You could consider this a side hustle for Bart. JB had an inside man working the outside. Follow me? Bart was introducing players to JB. Week in and week out, especially during football season they ran the Tuesday bank day together (I'll explain that later). Once debts were settled, Bart would get a cut of the action. Say you lost $100, once someone paid JB, Bart's virtual account would be credited a small percentage for just making the introduction and keeping the relationship going. The percentage per bet was small, but Bart had introduced like 50 or 60 guys over 5 years to the bookie and all of us players probably had a combined weekly action in the 10s of thousands. That small percentage wasn't chump change. And that was EVERY SINGLE WEEK!

Back to that phone call with Bart. After the introductory hello on the phone, he hit me with it. "What the hell are you doing?"

I noticed the slight chuckle and sensed an ease in his voice, but I also noticed the tone. It was a little sharp. What he was asking I wasn't sure of immediately, but I knew there was seriousness to his question.

"Did you really bet the over/under on the Rangers game?"

I answered, "Yup, it was 5 and a half." I continued, "The Rangers are one of the highest scoring teams and I thought playing their rivals across town (the Islanders), it would a high scoring game, I thought it would be a lock. Oh well, live and learn."

"Well, what did you learn?" Bart returned with.

Laughing, I responded with a sarcastic indirect true story. "Well, if you call the phone company and make a payment arrangement, they keep your phone on for up to two weeks."

That was the best way I could get my head around being broke again. All I had left was a good sense of humor. It was Monday morning and pay day (the day debts are settled is normally Tuesday each week) was in 24 hours, and again, I had just dumped my checking account on that hockey game. Since the Super bowl, going on almost two months, I haven't collected a dime. The NFL season was over and all I had left was the NBA and NHL. Both sports I didn't know much about.

I had made a joke about the phone bill, but it wasn't funny. I couldn't pay for it. I couldn't pay a handful of other bills either. I was in trouble and Bart probably knew it, too.

"I'll make you a deal, bud," Bart stated.

"Shoot," I replied.

"I'll cover your action last week, the full $3,000 from all this week's bets you currently owe if you can do me one thing."

"Sure." I had no idea where this was going, but I was intrigued, and he continued.

"Are you on your computer?"

"Nope!"

"Do you have the morning paper with you?"

Again, my answer, "Nope!"

"Perfect," Bart paused before continuing.

"Tell me the name, right now, of one player from the Rangers and one player from the Islanders? Go!"

Immediately there was an odd silence between us. I couldn't say anything. I was stuck in thought as I wasn't sure how to answer. It was the simplest question, but I had no reply. If he had asked me to name a player on the Broncos, I could name 80% of the team. The Cowboys or Buccaneers I could name about 50% of those players. Heck, I knew a good size of the Oklahoma Sooners roster by memory. His question about the two hockey teams though? I didn't have an answer to his question. It was the perfect question to uncover my problem.

After a brief silence, he spoke first. He was pleasant with his response, almost taking a brotherly demeanor, "That's what I thought."

Again, he continued before I spoke. "What in the hell are you doing betting that much money on a game that you have zero idea who is even on the ice?"

We went back and forth for probably another 20 minutes or so on the phone. It was a conversation that was required. Honestly, long overdue. Bart had always wanted me to win at everything I did or bet, unless it was against him, but my behavior towards betting was horrible. Bart had asked a question that I needed to hear; rather he asked a question that got me thinking for once.

What the hell am I doing betting on games that I have no idea who the players even are?

When I first got into betting the NFL and college football, pre-game research and homework were the only advantages you had. Obviously, I wasn't competing in the games myself; I had no direct ties to the teams or players, the only advantage was to possibly know something, anything, even just the slightest something that might give me an advantage. Bart had asked me that question because the night before I had just bet $500 on a hockey game and couldn't tell you one thing about either team. What he suspected was I couldn't even name a single player on either team.

And just like that, from one little call, I was off. Cold turkey, no warnings, or game plan, I was done. The question he asked was all I needed to hear. That and the fact I couldn't pay up that week also helped. J.B. just about drove me crazy collecting. It took three weeks for me to climb out of that hole. Once I made the last payment, I asked him to remove my number and never call me again. He honored that request.

I had to quit in that fashion, and I was damn glad to finally be out. After I spoke to JB Tuesday morning, we made some payoff arrangements and I also asked Bart to not deal me back in, ever again! Neither Bart nor JB had done anything wrong, but I wanted nothing more to do with wagering on anything ever again. I was 10 feet deep in a financial hole, AGAIN, but this time I was done for good.

# 3

# Off the Wagon

*"To succeed in life, you need two things:*
*ignorance and confidence."*
—Mark Twain

THE NFL TYPICALLY COMES OUT with the full season schedule each year in late spring for the following season. I believe most people that bet on games are fans first and gamblers second. I'd tell you I am the fan first kind of guy. I loved the game long before I ever placed a single bet. So, the first thing a fan does when say the Broncos schedule is released, is start making plans for the upcoming season. For me that might include what, if any, games I might try attending, what events around games in town or possibly on the road somewhere might grab interest or need some planning; and of course, what games I might, possibly, could be, should be placing a bet on. Good thing I quit gambling in March, wink wink.

I went the rest of spring that year and the entire summer without placing a single sports bet. I went to an Avalanche game or two. No betting at all. I was at maybe a dozen Rockies games that summer, no action. Years prior I was betting on boxing and MMA fights, and that summer "On the Wagon" Ronda Rousey was beating people up quickly. Yeah, that's a real name; she's one of the only ones I'll use in this book. Even though she's one of my favorite athletes I wasn't betting on her at all that summer. She started in Judo, my favorite martial art; and we both share the same birthday. I know, that's corny but years prior I bet every match she had. She had won me a small fortune, but that summer I was off (not betting) and was truly on top of my problem.

In years past after I memorized the Broncos schedule and made some tentative plans, that's about the time the problem gambler would come out. This year, I wasn't planning on what games to wager on, as I truly went into the new season for the first time in years not betting. Years prior I would look at not only the Broncos, but what other games looked appealing across the NFL schedule. Opening weekend of the NFL schedule is jammed packed full of action. The season kickoff Thursday night game was new in recent years but was overnight huge in popularity and of course with those who liked to wager. The Sunday night game and the Monday night game would also warrant some heavy consideration for where money was going, if that was your kind of thing.

Back in the early days of my experience with sports betting, I was given some advice worth noting for my story here. The best single piece of advice was to find a game each week that you think is a lock. Meaning, you can't lose! It doesn't always happen, but the amount of time I spent focusing on one game each week, year after year, meant something was working. I was told to keep away from your favorite teams. Too much emotion, those games couldn't be locks. Rather find a game or situation that looks off, or weird, or just something isn't right and follow it. See where it goes. If you do enough digging, and the lock looks good, try to capitalize on it. Once you find it, bet an amount comfortable for your wallet (I broke that part of the rule often). Anyway, that comfortable amount was there to keep the winning going, the streak alive, collecting a payoff in any amount was good for your mind and wallet. It's a mindset kind of tool. It's used in business and sports by top performers all the time. Ever hear the saying, "Never mess with a streak"? It's primarily used in baseball and good gamblers know this rule all too well. My problem was I'm not now or ever have been a good gambler. I'll never forget a game I found, a lock back in 2006.

Week three of the NFL season matched up division rivals New Orleans Saints vs. the Atlanta Falcons. The game was being played on Monday Night Football, which was already something special to most. The game carried a special meaning for the Saints. Probably beyond a special meaning for many reasons. The year prior, the Saints and the New Orleans community went through one of the worst Hurricanes on record, Hurricane Katrina. I know you, the reader, know of it. The storm did all kinds of unthinkable damage to the city and almost destroyed the Superdome where the Saints play. The damage was so bad, city officials had to decide if tearing the stadium down and rebuilding was an option. I read that it was almost a coin flip. They chose to repair what was already there, meaning in 2005 the Saints were without a home. They had to play their entire season away from their families, friends and fans of New Orleans.

Also going into the new season, the Saints had a new coach, and a new quarterback. Even though 2005 was rough, the Saints and the fans alike thought 2006 could be a turning point. A rebirthing some people called it. The Saints won only a couple of games in 2005, but everyone was talking about the Saints were a team on the rise and would possibly make the playoffs in 2006. A real dark horse, every gambler's love affair.

About mid-August that season, NFL pre-season time, I caught a video clip of their new franchise QB saying all the right things about his team, the city and of course a comment or two about the rebuilding of the Superdome. It was just a silly interview from some local news crew, but he made a comment I couldn't lose in my thoughts as the regular season got rolling. The reporter questioning him asked if there were any games on the schedule or possibly a certain team that he was looking forward to playing against. Immediately and without hesitation the QB answered, "Monday night, week three against the Falcons. Our home opener. I wouldn't bet against us!"

And with a smile, the QB walked off and the interview was over. Watching on TV mid-week during the preseason from my couch in Denver, I heard that message loud a clear. That interview was six weeks or so before that Monday night game. The Saints were playing on Monday Night Football, and the Dome was being re-opened that night. The city was using that weekend to re-launch New Orleans to the entire planet. We all knew of the hell that had visited a year earlier, somehow, I believe we were all rooting for the Saints and New Orleans. What we all didn't know is that QB knew something was up. They, the Saints, were going to whip the Falcons' butts that night.

So, I mentally noted the conversation I had witnessed and then waited. I was of course betting other games up to and including that weekend. Before I forget to mention, betting preseason football is the dumbest thing you can do by a 100-fold. I was already in the hole (down in money) when week three rolled around. Again, betting preseason football is the dumbest thing you can do, LOL. When the odds makers opened the lines (point spreads) the Saints were a home dog. Meaning the odds makers thought they were going to lose. The Falcons, being led by an all-star QB and heavily loaded team were four-point favorites to win. Still to this day, I wished I would have bet more. The closer to game time, the more confident I was. Four-point dogs though, at home? On Monday afternoon of game day, about three hours before kickoff, I made my bet. A straight up bet. No odds, no parlay, just a Saints win for $3,000. At the time, it was my biggest sports bet ever.

As the TV announcers started to talk about the game right before kickoff, the place was already exploding with energy.

You could hear it in the background through your TV as camera crews reported from both inside and outside the Superdome, you could sense something special was going to happen. It was probably the most comfortable I had ever felt about a bet in my life.

From kickoff until the final whistle, the Saints never trailed. Although they only won the game by 20 points, the score was never that close. The Saints beat the Falcons up and down the field. The city of New Orleans has often been considered as the largest party in America before Katrina. Until that Monday night game, there was a bit of uncertainty about how the city would respond. It only took that one game to let the world know, the city and Saints were back! The Saints were 3-0 in that season, and I was up $3,000. Life was good but for only a brief second.

Week four, just six days later, I went into the weekend with a full wallet and eyes on another big score. The Broncos had a bye that week, so I didn't have to wrestle with that betting plan. The first game I did bet was the Saints who were playing the lowly Carolina Panthers who were a struggling 1 and 2 team. No way coming off that huge game the weekend before could the Saints lose. I bet $1,000 on the Saints and you guessed it, they lost.

Game number two that weekend was another punch in the gut. Remember my story about finding a nugget of a game that you couldn't lose, a lock as it's called? Well, that game for me this week was the Browns against the Raiders. Both teams in 2006 for the week four game were winless. Yeah, they both were horrible and now were playing in the early-season toilet bowl. I remind you that I'm a Broncos fan and there are two rules for being a Broncos fan. The first is you are required to hate the Raiders. Period! That's easy. The second rule, under no condition, do you ever bet or even think of betting on the Raiders to win, EVER! I did all my homework, the Raiders were coming off an early season bye, the Browns were, and have always been, the Browns. They were not going on the road and beating the

Raiders. I broke one of my rules and that "lock" cost me another $1,000.

I bet on two other games that Sunday, each $500 and lost both. Six days prior I was up $3k and somehow rolling around to the Monday night game only a week later, I was back to even. I had bet it all back. The good news is that I could save my weekend as my other mini "lock" of the week was yet another Monday night game. This time in Philly. Odd, I thought, the week before while checking my future action. The upcoming Monday Night game featured the highest scoring team in the league, the Eagles, playing what could be an explosive team in the Packers, and the over/under was only 43 points? The Eagles themselves were averaging over 30 a game. The Packers had just posted two back-to-back weeks of almost 30. This is nuts, I thought Monday morning seeing the line set at only 43. I made my bet that afternoon of $1,500. I bet the over with just about as much confidence as the game in the Superdome the week prior. I went to the grocery store, got some fun eats and went home and got comfortable on my couch. Then proceeded to watch the Punt Bowl. Each team punted and punted and punted and punted themselves to a 31-9 final score. Neither team could do anything, including score. And just like that, I was down $1,500, again!

**********

Memories of 2006 and that Saints game is what drew me back in. I'd done all my homework, the game was under the radar, and nobody had caught a few things that a late-night TV news had broadcast. I knew the Saints would win and I had capitalized. That was then though. Now as the summer rolled along, I was determined to never make a sports bet again. Unfortunately, there was a lock creeping up in my mind that I couldn't let go.

As I had mentioned earlier, a lock shouldn't involve one of your favorite teams. It's bad business to bet with the emotion of it all. Gambling is a business, and businesses can't afford to be emotional. There is nothing worse than having your favorite team cost you. However, week one had an interesting match-up. It was one of the featured games of the week, and yes, it was on the sacred Monday Night Football.

A mere eight months earlier the Baltimore Ravens surprised the world and anyone who, say, bet heavy against them every single week of the playoffs (including the Super Bowl), by winning the entire thing. They cost me a ton of money. And wouldn't you know, they were making the return trip to face the Broncos and our Hall of Fame Quarterback on the first Monday Night game of the year.

That playoff loss was a tough pill to swallow for the entire Broncos team and all the fans in the Rocky Mountain region. Denver is a sports city built on the backs of the Broncos. We have all the major teams, and even a few other championships, but Denver is a football-first kind of town. I'm not sure about your town, but Denver bleeds orange first. And when the NFL released the schedule with Denver and Baltimore playing on that first Monday night game, even in the spring when I was battling the betting urge, in the back of my mind, I knew I was in trouble.

At the time, Denver had an all-pro receiver that the city loved, and our QB targeted often. If you played fantasy football, he was a top selected receiver in any league. It was mid-August of that upcoming season, and I was driving on my way to work. One of the local radio stations talks about the Broncos and the NFL almost non-stop. If you live in and around Denver, you know which radio station I'm talking about. Anyway, the radio personality was questioning our all-star receiver about random things. Mostly silly conversation just to fill airtime, but it was enjoyable. One of the questions asked was what he and the rest of the Broncos thought about their season debut against the Ravens, the same team that ended the prior season. He answered professionally and respectfully. I couldn't see the receiver's face, but through the airwaves his voice running across my dashboard speakers I could almost picture his grin. He had a few things to say during the interview, but the last thing he mentioned before the conclusion of the interview was, "I wouldn't bet against us." Being a fan, I loved hearing the comment. Being a gambler, I hated it.

Opening weekend went as planned. I hadn't placed a single bet on any game that weekend. I met a buddy for the Monday Night game for a burger and beer. For the first time in I can't remember how many years, I hadn't placed a bet on anything. The college season was in full swing, and I only watched about 12 hours that Saturday. Not a single wager. Sunday rolled around to another full day of talking on the phone with my dad and a few friends about the NFL and what we were watching. Nothing, no side action, not a single wager of any kind. I was determined to make it.

Monday, we kicked off the party a little early, like about 2:00. Much like everyone around town, we were all done working and were eager to get this game rolling. Everyone around town was ready for kickoff and for many, me included, some redemptions. The defending Super Bowl champions were in town, the same team that stole our Super Bowl the year prior. Payback was on everyone's mind, including mine.

I called LT (my new bookie) about an hour before kickoff. That's right, LT, not JB, more on that shortly. I'm not sure why, perhaps it's like a junkie calling his drug supplier. I've never done drugs, but an addiction is an addiction. I had been so good all summer, but perhaps this time around, I could control it, play within limits. Anyway, after the initial pleasantries, he asked what I wanted. Betting action, that is. I could hear the smugness in his voice. I had mentioned earlier that summer I was off, but he knew I'd be back. The asshole even joked about it on the phone. I didn't have much to say, we weren't friends. It was only business, or at least that's the way I wanted to keep it.

Finally, after the small talk I gave the instruction to open an account and that I would email my pick in shortly afterwards. I'd made up my mind. "Two-team parlay. Denver to cover, and the over." Officially and unfortunately, I was off the wagon......Again!

Denver won 49-27 that night. It was never that close. I started the season off with a bang and was up big from one bet in week one. The details of how and where my money went that year aren't important for my story here. In short, I kept betting Denver to win, and they kept winning. As they were pounding teams, the odds grew in the bookies' favor, not mine. To make some decent coin, you'd have to bet on long shots or parlays. All season I was up, but never very much. That all changed during the playoffs. Right before the holidays, I withdrew money from my online account and was positive in "football money" for the first time ever being a sports bettor.

Denver had home field advantage in the playoffs that year. After the divisional game against the Chargers, I was up again in my virtual account. The Patriots were coming to town for the Championship game, and I wasn't the least bit worried. I bet it all from the week's prior winnings, the Broncos took care of business and just like that I was up $4,800. Vegas was only two weeks away and I was going to bet every nickel on the Super Bowl. To say my confidence in the Broncos, and me winning a small fortune was at an all-time high, was an understatement.

# 4

# Survivor

*"The road to Easy Street goes through the sewer."*
—John Madden

As I JUST MENTIONED, both Bart and JB left me alone. Bart and I still chatted about other "life" things, sometimes even daily, but as far as betting, it was off limits. Unknowingly, Bart had even actually helped me with my last debt owed to JB. JB, who was a nice guy, didn't strike me as the most organized businessman. After my last hockey wager, JB had called with payoff instructions. I couldn't do the entire amount, and we worked out an arrangement. On the last week of that arrangement, he had called inquiring to what checking account I was to pay into (That fun little detail coming). The total remaining balance I was quoted due, well it was the wrong total.

I didn't argue, it was in my favor, so after I paid up that next Friday and that was the end of my relationship with JB. My only relationship with him was with sports betting so to this day, I haven't had a single word with him. Bart had his own issues with gambling, and I secretly think he was glad I was off so his getting off betting would be easier for him as well. I found out years later, that JB called Bart on that last week and wasn't sure of what my total owed was. Bart said it was something less than what I owed. Bart was a good friend and found an opportunity to help a pal out.

This is the part where I bring Larry into the story. Otherwise known as LT, as I previously mentioned. These guys all use initials and nicknames as part of their "hiding," but I know LT's real name was Larry. He was from Texas, and you'd never believe how I met this guy. Bart didn't know about this guy, or at least the fact he was booking bets. I told nobody about him. Meeting him assured me I would go in the wrong direction with sports betting. After saying goodbye to JB, I started betting with LT far too soon. Starting back up was an issue, now I was trying to do it in complete darkness, which would be another issue down the road.

So how did I meet Larry, AKA LT? Well back in college, a group of us, yes Bart was there, we started a fantasy football league. 1990 was the actual year. We were there drafting players long before the internet sites like today. We drafted an entire defense by position. Our teams were 40 players deep and the record keeping was based solely off the Monday morning newspaper. It was super fun if you didn't have to do the points and record keeping. My God, that was a nightmare.

Anyway, the second year of our league we had a new player, a friend of ours who would introduce us all to something else, another form of gambling. His name.... let's see, we will call him Michael. On draft night for the Fantasy league, Michael was over at the draft house, and we all drafted our teams. Of course, we had a poker game planned afterwards and during that game, Mike asked, "Have you guys ever heard of a Survivor League?"

None of us had, but it was gambling, and we were in. A Survivor League in some circles also is called a Last Longer League, Suicide Pool, One and Done, or even The Last Loser. The rules are very simple. You come up with a one-time entry fee.

That night we had eight of us and we all paid $25 which gave us a $200 pot. It was the winner take all. No cash up front, no action in the rear; meaning you had to pay before game one, week one. If you didn't start the season at week one, you couldn't get in mid-season. The only other important rule was each week of the NFL season you pick one team to win. That's it. Through the season, you can never pick the same team twice, so some strategy certainly comes into play as the NFL season goes on. If you select a loser at any time, you are out. No more for fun the rest of the NFL season. Sounds easy, doesn't it? Well, it's beyond tough, and super frustrating.

As you move forward each week, not only do you need to of course pick a winner, but you need to start plotting a winning course weeks in advance. Who's on the road, who's hot, and who's not? Maybe a coaching change mid-season or a freak blizzard in Buffalo might lean you towards a pick away from a warm weather Miami team. You could strategize a pick, several weeks down the road and maybe a late week injury before kickoff could change that strategy. As the weeks progressed, it became harder and harder to pick a winner.

In all my years playing in this league, with many of the original guys, I rarely got past mid-season. That was until the 2006 NFL season. In the years prior, I wasn't alone as the attrition rate was about 25-30% of the teams would drop out each and every week. Some weeks we might only lose say 5-10% of the players, but other weeks, we'd lose 30-40%. One particular year, the New England Patriots were playing a rotten New York Jets team and were like 14-point favorites. Half our league thought they had a lock, and you guessed it, we lost half the players in our league the first week of the season. In 2006, that one year alone, we were down to less than 170 teams midway through the season. I forgot to mention, our little college league had grown just a tad. Anyway, back in 2006, I can't remember the games, but around Thanksgiving a couple "lock" teams had around 150 teams pick them to win and of course, the locks all lost. In one weekend, we were down to under 20 teams in the league. It was getting serious now for a couple of reasons.

First, as I just hinted, the league had been growing steadily, every year since its inception. A few years earlier, the league entry fee had changed and now we were charging $100 per team. Another rule change is you could have just a single team, or if you wanted to have several teams in the same league, no problem. It would cost $100 for each. We had several guys who had 5, 6, 7 and I believe we had one guy who invested in 10 teams for an entry of $1,000. In 2006, our little college league had grown to over 2,400 teams, each paying $100. If you can do basic math, you already know that our Survivor League was worth $240,000+ and I was still alive, late in the season.

So, December rolls around and things are getting interesting. Not only is the upcoming week critical, but teams play a little differently in December than they do in October. Some teams are heading into the playoffs, others are heading to vacation. Some players are playing for future contracts, various coaches are on hot seats, and of course, the weather all over the country is playing havoc on running teams versus throwing teams. All of which means your selection each week is planned, reviewed, plotted, scrutinized, and changed at least a dozen times throughout the week.

Week 12, I picked a winner. Week 13, I nailed the winner again and we lost 4 more teams in the league. Going into week 15, we had 16 teams remaining, all battling for our share of the $240,000. For the first time all year, I thought about what it would be like to win or at least get a share. Even if it wasn't for the full amount, a 16-way chop would pay over $15,000 tax free, and oh God did I need that money.

We received the weekly updates, spreadsheet, predictions and sports talk from Michael via email. It was something he did each and every week and he had done it without fail, for years actually. On Tuesday each week, he'd send out the spreadsheet with who made it another week. This time, only 16 teams received the emails. He'd spare the other teams that had lost from receiving a worthless email. Anyway, I think the email from Michael came in about 11:00 a.m. Maybe about a half hour later, we all received an email from another guy who was also still a survivor. I didn't know the person, but his email was simple. "Guys, wanna make a deal?"

Deals in gambling are simple and happen often. When the prize pool starts getting close for the remaining players, often deals are negotiated to assure some kind of win for everyone. Why go that far and not make some money. I was in, and so were about 13 other guys. We all thought making a deal was smart, but 2 guys, however, held out. The emails between all us survivors went back and forth for the next few days. Nobody else was included in the conversation that wasn't still in the league. I think on Wednesday there must have been 200 emails bouncing around between everyone who was still in. Negotiating, pleading, discussing, arguing, and in some cases begging. To be honest, it all got pretty silly. One guy who was still in it, was named Larry (AKA LT). I didn't know him yet, but it was through this Survivor league that I met him, my future next bookie.

He had sent out an email to the group of 16 and I inadvertently answered having only copied him. It started communication between just the two of us which led to us exchanging phone numbers. We formed a kind of a friendship and were discussing a split between just the two of us for whatever amount that we might be winning, just to protect a potential payout for the both of us. Translated, if we both finished out the season winning, we would take our shares and that would be it. If one of us won, and the other lost in the remaining two weeks, the loser would still be in for a chunk of the other guy's payout. We agreed to an 80/20 split, winner to loser. All we needed was one of us to win out, and we'd both be in the money.

That was a good plan. Collecting money is still collecting money. We also agreed that we'd keep our pick quiet, so the other guy didn't say or do anything to influence a change. There's nothing worse than giving your buddy advice on a bet and in essence changing his mind and being wrong. I did it one time and convinced a pal to change his mind and it almost led to a fist fight between friends. Never again, and LT agreed. There could only be one problem with our little side deal though.

If we both picked the same team and that team lost, we'd both be out of any potential payout. With 16 games, and several-odd possible playoff implications, what are the odds? I wasn't worried, nor was LT. There were a couple of lame matchups, and for being late in the year, weather wasn't an issue in any of the games I was looking at. Two weeks prior to week 15, I was eyeing a game, and my pick hadn't wavered. Now two weeks later, on Monday morning after having won week 14, I was 99% sure who I was going with, but still didn't send in my pick until Friday. I took my time, did the research, checked with the on-line sites and watched which direction all the Vegas casinos were going.

I came up with a lock. A team I thought couldn't lose. Everyone still left in the league would find out later, that of the 16 teams remaining in week 15, 12 teams chose the same NFL team. LT included. Do I even need to tell you what happened?

LT and I spoke late Sunday night, both of us almost in tears. Misery loves company and we spoke for about 45 minutes about the loss. Not the game really, but more about the loss in winnings. It's fair to say we were good company that night. A week earlier I was fantasizing about winning $240k. A few days ago, I had secured what I thought would be at minimum a few thousand. Monday morning, the next day, I woke up with no future "bonus" money coming in. At the time, I was betting with JB and had mentioned this to LT during that conversation. LT of course immediately jumped on that opportunity and offered his "services" if I ever wanted to make a bet. How convenient and odd meeting him in this fashion.

The remaining four teams all correctly picked a winner in week 16. Each team that year evenly split the prize pool. I didn't know anyone who received a payout, but each survivor had better than $60,000 coming their direction. What a great year-end bonus. I was so bummed, so distracted for a week with "what-if" thoughts, it was hard to work. I would later find out what a blessing it was not cashing in that year.

The league ended abruptly the following year. And with a bang did it ever end. The following football season, we had another strong enrollment. Better than 2,800 teams from around the country, roughly 30 +/- states had guys playing. Again, I purchased one single team and called them the Headhunters. In week one, another "lock" was picked by 1,100 of those teams, not me, I had learned my lesson, and you guessed it. The lock lost, and our league was almost cut in half the first game of the season. Oh, were some of the emails and stories flying around that following week a thing of beauty. It still makes me laugh to this day every time I think of it. Anyway, the original group all agreed that Michael had to take a cut. He was managing over a quarter a million dollars, sending out updates and a spreadsheet each week. The governing body made up of mostly the guys who started the league agreed to pay him 3% of the total pool. In the grand scheme of things that was well worth it, and he did do a great job. Always reliable, on time, and he managed it like a real business.

On or about week five that year, my team was already out. I had picked an iffy team a week or two prior and now was only spectating. At about the same time oddly, Michael had also disappeared. No emails, no weekly reminders, spreadsheets, nothing. For the first time ever, his communication was gone. The first week of his absence, nobody thought much about it. Me and a handful of guys who spoke often, just brushed it off.

Another week passed and now a few guys were starting to reach out to other circles. He wasn't returning emails, text messages, and now his phone was off. Did he drop dead or something? This was not like him; it was beyond odd. Somebody mentioned something silly, but perhaps this guy took off with almost $300k in our Last Longer Pool? After the third week of silence, many guys started digging.

A few guys close to Michael were warned to back off and it was quietly mentioned to spread word to anyone else looking to also back off and not inquire what was going on. Warned from whom though? We were told that everyone needed to stop with the phone calls and emails. All that was said was there wasn't a lot that could be said, and even less should be talked about. Personally, I had already lost that season, but now morbid curiosity kept me checking into things on my end. In essence, it had been another two months and Michael, and the league's money disappeared without a word. There was lots of grumbling. Some guys kept sending in their picks. Others said to heck with it, others even against the warnings kept digging into where Michael and the prize pool had gone.

I guess him having died would have been the worst news, but that wasn't it. What did happen was a close second, and when a near friend to Michael leaked out some information everyone in the league did their best Texas two-step to distance themselves from the league.

Apparently, one fall day early in our football season, in an office park somewhere in America, Michael stepped out for lunch with a client. He ignored the calls from the office, but didn't ignore the text message received stating, "911 - call the office immediately!" The rumor I heard was the message read "Call the office now!!! Worse than 911."

I can only imagine the horror as your mind would go nuts just reading such a text. I heard that he excused himself away from the lunch table and made the call. His receptionist answered, and then immediately handed the phone to the law enforcement officer waiting back at his office. I'm not 100% sure, but I think it was a sheriff's officer there to arrest him. I guess there were four men in total. Two local officers, one person from the justice department and you guessed it, one IRS agent. He was told if he didn't want to come to the office, they would happily head to his home and arrest him there in front of his wife and children.

We never heard from Michael again. Nobody! Almost like a ghost, he just disappeared. The league and the money were gone, and nobody went farther down that road. We heard rumors of a job loss as he was doing the league's spreadsheets on a company computer and sending out gambling information from a company computer as well. Oops. It was a good job; his career, and it paid well. But that wasn't the worst. We also heard rumors of gambling crime charges, wire, money and banking laws charges and of course all kinds of IRS issues. If you are reading this Michael, I truly am sorry for the hell you must have gone through. I never heard where it all ended, but I can only imagine the worst.

One last little detail that probably needs mentioning. Remember the year prior when I almost went the distance and received my portion of the $240k? Well, sometimes God's best gifts are unanswered prayers. I had prayed to win my share of that money, and it didn't happen.

Part of Michael's process, when in the hands of the legal system, is that he had to turn over all persons who had received a cash payout in prior years. That included the prior year and those that had won the $240k prize money. I'm sure the four remaining teams from the year prior all had visits from the IRS! Ouch.

Anyway, back to the Broncos and the Super Bowl run. I was up $4,800 going into Superbowl Sunday. I think I bet on 10 or 11 games that year on the Broncos and only missed maybe once. I did leave a few tough weeks alone. What a great feeling to be in control that way. LT had called on Tuesday after the Broncos beat the Pats and asked where and how I wanted my payout. "Keep it for now," I instructed him. The Broncos, having won and now in route to the Super Bowl, had delivered twice for me with wins; and the other games over the past couple weeks padded my virtual bank account nicely.

Monday morning, the day after the AFC championship game, a few of us started working on Vegas plans for the big game. I had won every bet I placed in the post season. The only game I was off was the over in the AFC Championship. Thanks Denver! LOL. One more win, a win on Denver in the Super Bowl would cap off a great season of winning sport betting. It would have been great to make the trip to New York but an outdoor game back East during the dead of winter didn't sound half as much fun as Vegas did. It started off with just a couple of us, but by the end of the workday, we had nine guys committed to going. A couple of good pals that I worked with and a few others we all knew.

Vegas was going to be something most guys only dream of. The week prior to leaving, we established a couple of rules. First, as soon as we got on the plane the Friday before, anyone who brought up anything about work the entire weekend would pay heavily in bar tabs. Second, no wives, girlfriends, or anything else were allowed to go that could interrupt our guy's weekend. Yea, cheesy, but a rule's a rule. Nothing was permitted that might disrupt the fun and games. The third and final rule? Whatever happens, Deny, Deny, Deny!

# 5

# What's Your Story?

*"The happiness of your life*
*depends upon the quality of your thoughts."*
—Marcus Aurelius

BEFORE CONTINUING WITH THE SUPER BOWL MELTDOWN, I need
to tell you how all this mess all began. How did I ever venture
down this road and end up here? I ask myself that often and
both laugh and sometimes almost cry at times just thinking of
things. Every event, or rather "story" in our lives has come to
life from someplace. Regardless of the thrill of victory, or the
agony of defeat, all our stories began and have ultimately landed
somewhere. The successful stories result from having a well
laid out plan that perhaps has been executed to perfection from
inception to finality. Others though, are all over the board from
some version of successes to complete failures. All of them share
a characteristic that anyone's story has come from someplace.
This is where "my story" came from.

It was the spring of 1983. We had an elder family member
pass away and my immediate family was on the road the next
day to Albuquerque, New Mexico. My immediate family was
Mom, Dad, and two younger brothers. The dog stayed home with

a large bowl of food. The extended family wasn't all that much larger. Add all of them and the friends from here and there, and we might have had 50-60 people in town for services that day.

Now most of the family and most of those friends of the recently departed were all Southerners. If you don't know what a "Southerner" is, perhaps another nickname and you'll understand. Southern Engineer, Hillbilly, Country, Boo, Beau, Buck, and everyone's favorite, Redneck. These and many more alike are labels often planted on someone for God knows whatever reason. I mention this, as often people understand "Southerners" or "Rednecks" do things a little differently. Our family, being from the South, did do things a little off, and yes, a funeral wasn't an exception.

After the hubbub at the cemetery, the family would get together for a feast that resembled a national holiday or a Super Bowl party. Often some kind of BBQ, baked beans and hot wings you could come to expect. Alcohol was normally in ample supply for the adults and the sneaky older teens.

Soon the day passed into night, and so did remembering and honoring the dead. What were glum hours speaking of memories and shedding a few tears turned into a night filled with fun and laughter. Rednecks are weird, so the idea of having family together shouldn't be wasted on loss alone. Funerals are a time to celebrate the dead, and for most of the family, celebrating was exactly what the family was going to do.

As the sun set and turned to night, many of the adults cleared the kitchen table and broke out a deck of cards. At that moment, I had no idea what game they were going to play. The mood was good; people were telling jokes and laughing. I didn't need an invitation, whatever was going on, I was in.

I was there in the kitchen talking with an uncle of mine. Let's call him Scooter. I haven't spoken with him in years, but I think that was his real nickname. He was twice my age, but we could speak like best buds. We continued chatting as my mom drug about eight or so chairs from all over the house, one at a time and sat them around the kitchen table. The table looked barely big enough to sit four, maybe five adults. Before I had a chance to ask Scooter what they were going to do, my mother barked out an invitation, if that's what you want to call it.

"Penny-ante poker, boys! Who's in?"

Scooter, when asked if he wanted to play a little poker nodded his head and grinned from ear to ear. I had no clue what kind of game poker was, but by the way the other adults also started grabbing for open seats, I was guessing this might be something fun. I found a folding chair and sat it right behind Scooter so I could watch. The games began, and I never missed a hand. I was immediately Scooter's biggest fan, and he was my hero at the table.

A hero not because of what he had accomplished on the poker table. Rather, he teased me all night with a view into this adult world. I thought he was the coolest guy for letting me have a view into the world of gambling. Scooter sat there for the first hour whispering over his shoulder what was going on. He would peel up the corner of his cards so I could have a look. When he wasn't directly involved with a hand, he'd lean back and explain what hands beat what. He tried to predict what other players had based on how they played, or rather how they bet. He called those tells.

It was roughly an hour before I had the basics down. Straights are good, but they don't beat flushes. Often the hands are won early by aggressive betting and if you happen to get a full house, punish the other players who remained. Get every dime you can, anytime it presented itself. A royal flush is the best hand in the game, but Scooter told me you could wait a lifetime before you get a royal.

As the night proceeded, Scooter and I became partners. Of course he didn't know it, but his student, me, wanted a part of this game. Although it was for adults only, nobody around the table seemed to care I was playing his hands. Occasionally he would ask mid-hand what I wanted to do? My response was normally, raise, re-raise, and occasionally I'd have the opportunity to declare all-in! Even though I was bluffing a lot, I never wanted to show weakness, and I rarely ever folded. That was of course the easy way to play. I wasn't playing with my own money.

Sometime after midnight the game ended, and it was time for bed. What a horrible feeling. I wanted more of this nonsense. Scooter, though, was happy for the game to end. Having his biggest fan, me, in his ear all night cost him every dollar in his wallet.

I was fascinated by the mechanics of the game. The fairness of it all, while at the same time how unfair and cruel the game could be from hand to hand. Poker loves everyone and at the same time favors nobody. The joy or feeling of winning is only matched by the pain of losing. I could have sat there for three days and not eaten or slept playing that night in Albuquerque. Scooter told me that in both Vegas and kitchen tables around the world, that's exactly what gamblers do. Was I a future gambler? I didn't know then, but I wouldn't see another live game until my freshman year in college, some five plus years later.

It was October 1988, and I was at the University of Northern Colorado in Greeley. It was my freshman year. I was there to play college football, chase girls and occasionally go to class. I was there studying business, then psychology, then criminal justice. Truth be told, studying wasn't the top of my normal daily to-do list. I'm not sure of the exact date, but I know it was a Friday in October. It was a chilly fall day, and I had no assignments due, nor tests to take, thus the day was nothing but mine to do whatever I wished.

Bart (yup the same guy), waltzes into my room unannounced as usual. He was wearing a tee-shirt and tightie whities, that's all. We were suite mates assigned to adjoining rooms our freshman year. He was at first a stranger, and then would later become one of my better friends. He was also the one who introduced me later in life to JB. You've already read about that.

It was roughly noon, and I was still in bed. He was standing in the little foyer in my dorm room and asked. "Bro, you ever play poker?"

I hadn't thought about the game since Scooter's introduction several years prior. I was a decent student in high school and a slightly better athlete. My mind was in many other areas during high school. To be honest, the game of poker rarely even crossed my mind to play or try to get a game together. However, the second Bart mentioned the word poker, I sprang out of the bed like the building was on fire. Twenty minutes later, we had rounded up enough guys to start the game.

That first game started twenty minutes past noon that Friday in a dorm room next door. We sat on the floor and pitched cards amongst smelly feet and college guys barely dressed. Most of us were just waking. Those that did have afternoon classes immediately cancelled that silly plan. Why go to class when there's a poker game going on? Nobody had brushed their hair, their teeth and some hadn't showered in three days, maybe longer. We weren't the characters and living the same life as those from the movie Animal House, but we were a close second.

I kid you not, that first game lasted for three days. Exactly what Scooter had mentioned years prior that gamblers do. For three straight days, we played every version of every game known to man. Some of us were a little better player than others, but we all took turns winning and losing. Not necessarily by choice, but rather by the odds of the game. The game of poker has a weird way of keeping things close. As bad as your bankroll might be, you always just thought one more hand and you'd be back to even.

That weekend we ordered pizzas and ate junk food. We left the dorm floor long enough to visit the bathroom and that was it. My girlfriend, Julie, stopped by on Saturday at some point, I can't even come close to remembering if it was day or night, but what I do remember was that she just about passed out from the smell. She said the room smelled like being trapped in a plastic outhouse. Oddly I remember, I didn't smell a thing.

I think by Monday morning, around 4 a.m., we finally called it quits. After all, some of us did have classes on Monday a few hours later. Those of us who didn't, or had decided to skip class, needed a little sleep and some of us needed some money. Money was an entirely different adventure for anyone in college, much less kids who played cards.

In just three short days, guys were going broke. Some quit, others kept pressing on and turned to paying with IOU's. Having been there and paid like that, we quickly ended that BS. Playing for IOU's was not how we were going to go forward. We made people come with money, so if you didn't have any, you had to figure it out. If you got into a game that bankrupted you during the game, you had to pay right then and there. What various guys figured out was way worse.

In one particular game, we played a wild card game that got progressively bigger during the hand. If you were playing badly or had bad luck, this game could drain your wallet mid-hand. Well, it happened, and to one of the better players. There was one guy who played poker fairly well, but he ran into some bad luck on this one particular hand. He lost every dollar he had on him and owed the pot another $80.

It was only $80, but that was a small fortune in college. We all marveled at what had just happened and laughingly demanded he settle up before being dealt into the next hand. He left the room and was back two minutes later. He laid down $20 in cash for more chips, and gave the winner of the prior pot, the one he just lost to, a stack of textbooks. "Valued at re-sale for better than a $100 he claimed. "Take these and sell them at the campus bookstore." He stated. It was a good deal. The winner got his money, plus some, and we had a player back, and his $20 bucks got him back in the game.

That was our freshman year. Every guy on our floor and others around campus had spent the better part of 50-60 hours a week playing poker on a dorm room floor that year. We barely broke for anything else. It was a rare event to get anyone away from card room central. Heck, my girlfriend Julie once came in the room sometime that spring upset with me about something and broke up with me. Right in front of everyone, the room stunned in silence, everyone waiting for my reaction, I didn't move a muscle and only said what first came to mind. "Whose turn is it to deal?"

After the spring semester was complete, we all headed home for what was a necessary break. I didn't play a single hand of poker that following summer. I couldn't get into casinos yet legally and most of the guys in our poker circle in college lived far enough away that it really wasn't worth trying to get a game going. We all did work and thus built up our bankrolls.

That fall, we all had different pads across town in Greeley. It was for most of us, our second year in college. There to study and learn something. Oh, we learned various things alright. Primarily how to survive the whims of college. Some of us rented houses, others an apartment here and there. A few guys roomed together, while others had a new friend come in the mix. We all, though, played poker.

As the games got better with talent, they also got bigger in scale of money. What was once nickel, dime, and quarter pots in most of our games, in some cases got to be in the hundreds, if not a couple games with thousands in the pot. None of the players playing could afford that action. The rush poker could bring to your psyche, the possibility of a big win, all of it, was worth the gamble though. This is the point I need to include two unusual games that we started playing.

One guy in our group had lost a pot he couldn't afford. He

was only in the pot with a hand that should have been a lock for the win. It was a wild card game, and he really got screwed by an unbelievable rare outcome. Not in his favor of course, and against all odds, you'd call that a bad beat. He lost a pot he shouldn't have, a big one, and didn't have the money to settle. Everyone not in the hand thought it was hilarious. His offer to the winner to "settle up" was historic.

"How about if you let me out of that debt, I let you spank my ass with that ping pong paddle?"

That was rather an odd offer and completely random. Immediately the winner of the pot, renegotiated back. Like a well-trained stock trader looking for an investment opportunity, "I'll let you out of the debt, but everyone here at the table gets to have one swat!"

And just like that, "Lose Your Ass," a different kind of poker game was born. We played poker just like before, but this time, if you played a pot and couldn't settle up, everyone playing in the game got a swat with you bent over the couch. Oddly, it became the preferred method of commerce. If a pot was small, a whack on your pal's ass was always better than winning a few bucks. We allowed various tools. Your hand, a flip-flop, wooden spoon perhaps, and yes, a ping pong paddle. We didn't even have a ping pong table, how that ever made it into the room was never known.

We even played entire nights without money. How sick is that? We played for hours on end and the only winner was whoever had his ass beat the least. Losing your ass took on a whole new meaning. We had guys running from across the room trying to add force to their swat. Guys were trying to use the little they learned in physics to jump off other furniture to get a better angle for the swat. Anything you could come up with to administer more pain. Oddly, we had girlfriends, and other random coeds coming for a seat in the game. What the hell? Everyone took turn losing their ass!

The reality though, that game started to hurt. Physically. My ass was so sore a few nights, sitting on the toilet the next day took on a whole new meaning. All the humor and sickness of beating another's back side was hilarious and all, but after a bad run of cards, you might not be able to sit again for an hour. Just about that time, our newest game was proposed, and "Stunt Poker" came to life.

It was simple. We played cards games just like always. It could be a straight up game, or a game with wild cards, multiple draws, whatever. It was poker, with a catch. The punishment for losing wasn't handing off your money or offering your ass for a spanking. It was a predetermined stunt. We'd come up with some little stunt, that if you lost, you had to perform right then and there.

Of course, the stunts started off rather easy. Early on in our stunt poker days we'd have to chug a beer or down three shots before the next hand. That was easy. Another stunt was you had to eat two tablespoons of raw hamburger meat if you lost. That was rough. It wasn't very long before some version of nudity and running around campus was the norm. If MTV and video cameras were around my sophomore year, we would have all been the first members of Jackass!

And that's the way it was for the better of five years or so in college. Over the next few years, we had the bulk of the original crew intact for each game. Others would come and go. In later years we mixed it up. Some Lose Your Ass, a little Stunt Poker here and there, but the norm returned to cash games.

Gambling was legalized in Colorado in the fall of 1990 while I was in college. Oddly, its first year in operation was my 21st year, making me legal. I was finally able to legally gamble and play cards at an entirely different level. I hadn't ever bet a sports bet in a casino or with a bookie, but that was soon to come.

# 6

# Abu

*"Anyone who lives within their means*
*suffers from a lack of imagination."*
—Oscar Wild

FAST FORWARD TO SPRING OF 2003, my grandmother called one day to say hello. We were just a few seconds into our conversation when I realized there was another motive for the call. Grandma was calling to ask me for a favor. "Shawn, can you please come get your grandfather out of the house?" She continued after I asked if everything was alright. "He's fine, just grumpy and a tad stir-crazy. He hasn't left the house all winter."

I was very close with my grandparents. They were more or less an extension of my parents. If you had to picture them, my grandfather was an "Archie Bunker" kind of guy. A WWII Navy Veteran who at one point owned a trucking company listed on the New York Stock Exchange. Not bad for a guy that didn't finish junior high school.

My grandmother was a mix of Wilma Flintstone and Esther from the *Sanford and Son* TV series. She was a bit of polite, kind, God-fearing, and punch-you-in-the-mouth kind of woman that everyone loved, but equally feared when you had done something wrong. She and Gramps (as I called him until the day he died) had two kids. My grandmother passed prior to Gramps; they had made it 62 years in marriage.

Anyway, back in that spring she and I agreed that I would pick Gramps up Saturday morning and the two of us were going to Black Hawk to play some poker. Black Hawk is a little gaming town about 30 miles outside of Denver. I had only played with Gramps maybe once or twice before in the prior years but really, since having started my own family, I hadn't played cards more than a dozen times in the past five years or so with anyone. It just wasn't my thing then or a priority. My wife was super cool with me going that day. And just like looking forward to an upcoming vacation, I was very much looking forward to it several days prior.

That Saturday rolled around quickly and by 8 a.m., we had already made the 45-minute drive to Black Hawk. It was a sunny and warm, spring Colorado day. If we weren't playing poker, it would have been a great day to go fishing. However, we were playing cards, and we had somehow managed to play at the same table, side by side no less. From the start you could just feel it was going to be a great day. Both of us were happy to be spending time together and doing so while playing cards. When one of us was out of a hand, the other would peel the corner of the cards in a fashion to let the other see what cards they held. If we happened to both be in a pot and one of us had a very strong hand, a gentle foot tap under the table notified the other that you had a solid hand. We never wanted to take the other's money.

We ended up playing for the better of 10 hours. That wasn't the original plan. What I had told the wife is that we would be home in maybe 5 or 6 hours. I think we told Grandma the same thing. That was also back in 2003 when cell phones weren't a thing yet and the casino had one pay phone. Not that it mattered as I couldn't tell you now, much less then, where it might be. We didn't call either of our wives to alert them we were going to be late.

I dropped Gramps off after a successful day in the casino, and after the butt chewing from Grandma. I started the 30-minute trip home for probably what was going to be another butt chewing. I asked my grandmother to call my wife and alert her that I was on the way. Grandma quickly and sarcastically told me that the two of them had already spoken and I was in for it. Oh, how I love women.

On the way home, I was trying my best to come up with a good story for why we were so late. The song *Dreams* by Van Halen was on the radio, and I had a quick chuckle thinking of an oldie Gramps had told me years prior. Perhaps if I delivered correctly when I got home, it could help my cause.

The joke goes that this married man was having an affair with his secretary. The two would leave the office at different times of the day and head to a hotel, perhaps, or maybe they would plan a fun lunch back at her place. They had been involved for a few months when they decided to take one afternoon off after lunch and have a "fun" time back at her place. Well sometime late that afternoon, they feel asleep and didn't awake until early evening. He was late, had already missed dinner and hadn't called prior to tell his wife he'd be home late. He was in big trouble, maybe on the verge of being caught.

After awakening, he immediately jumped out of bed with his secretary/girlfriend and instructed her to quickly take his nice work shoes and go run them through, in, and around the flower garden. He instructed her not to forget to rub them in the grass out in the front yard as well. "Quickly, make them dirty, the dirtier the better." He requested this urgently. She was off and running while he re-dressed.

About a minute later he was out in the front yard putting on his grass and dirt-stained shoes on the front porch. The man gave his lady a kiss goodbye and sped off towards home. He knew his wife would be upset and would be waiting for his arrival.

Twenty minutes later, just as the man feared, he rounded the corner into his neighborhood and from a distance he could see his wife waiting at the front door. The scowl on her face was frightening even at a distance. Her arms were folded across her chest and the man noticed an impulsive slight tap of her front foot. Oh, she looked pissed for sure. As he pulled into the driveway, she started walking out towards him, ready for battle.

"Where the hell have you been?" she barked out.

"Hun, I'm going to tell you the truth," he responded as she waited for a reply.

He paused for a brief second maybe two, looked her square in the eyes and gulped possibly his last breath before admitting, "Honey, I'm having an affair!"

The wife paused, shook her head in disbelief and continued her verbal assault towards her husband.

"You are a lying SOB. I see your shoes! You've been golfing again!"

As much as I enjoyed that joke, it probably wasn't going to work. I knew my wife was going to be pissed at me being so late. I probably ran through that one and another joke a dozen times in my head before getting home. And as expected, I immediately got an earful upon walking inside the house. I didn't even try the humor route. She wasn't going to hear any of the nonsense.

What I did was apologize, sincerely. I told her that we had so much fun, it was even harder to leave at the time we did. I also asked her to call my grandmother and tell her how much fun I had had with Gramps. You know, make them both feel even better by suggesting I get out of the house myself. I wasn't sure if she was necessarily following me in the moment, but as I opened my wallet and she glanced at the ten extra hundred dollar bills, well the mood improved dramatically. Funny how seeing cash can do exactly that.

And that's how it restarted again. Back playing poker that is. The family and my career were more important. Over the course of the next year, my personal life would see many changes.

Things I didn't see coming, and some things I certainly didn't plan for either.

About a month after that day playing poker with Gramps, I took a little four-day trip with a couple of college buddies to New Orleans. We were heading to The Final Four; college basketball's yearly party to celebrate the best in college hoops, was playing in the Big Easy. I'd been to the Superdome for a Broncos game before, but this was my first college basketball tournament. It was a bucket list item, and the wife blessed me with a hall pass.

Just like typical tourists, we did all the New Orleans "checklist" items. Once we landed, the party had begun. For four days, we were constantly on the move. We spent some time on Bourbon Street. We spent A LOT of time on Bourbon Street. We hit almost every bar on that street and many of the bars on side streets as well. We ate all around town and drank each day like we were competing for some kind of Olympic medal. Some days if I remember correctly, we were having drinking contests amongst ourselves and random strangers from all over the world. It was the most I had drank since college many years prior.

Of course, the reason for being down there was for the basketball games and the events or functions surrounding the games. But I can't imagine the Final Four in another city being as wild as this party was down here in the Big Easy. It was complete nuts! At times I swear we only needed a deck of cards and a ping pong paddle, and we could have started a Lose Your Ass poker game right smack dab in the middle of town. I couldn't even imagine a Stunt Poker game down there. Someone would have died!

If you haven't been to New Orleans, you are missing out. If you have been, you know exactly what I'm talking about. Now mix that memory with 30,000 college-aged students and BAM.... hysteria. In the middle of Bourbon Street one night, we stumbled onto a unique little store in the middle of town.

It was some random store with a mixture of BBQ sauce,

Voodoo trinkets, tee-shirts, liquor, shot glasses, post cards, stuffed alligator heads, everything! It had something for everyone. If you couldn't find a gift in there, the gift didn't exist. Without a doubt it was one of the strangest shops I've ever been into, and New Orleans isn't short on strange shops.

Before leaving the store, one of guys working behind counter came from around back and darted directly towards me. His haste was obvious. It was easily a 20-foot distance or so and the direction he was heading was towards me. Without introduction he questioned, "Sir, you have an amazing aura. If I give you a discount, would you please let our spiritualist do a reading on you?"

This is probably one of those moments that I should have questioned the man with a few things prior to agreeing. What I should have questioned was maybe what the hell is an aura? Or what is a spiritualist? A reading you say, what in the world is that? I wasn't clear on any of these and before I knew what was going down, I was being led to the back of the store and down a dimly lit hallway. I wasn't even sure I responded yes to any of this, and I wasn't even sure how much this "reading" was going to cost at this point.

At the end of the narrow, poorly lit, hallway was a bead door. Yup, I was walking towards the 1970s. Through the beads I could hear some lite music playing softly on a scratchy record player. The room was brown and red. Everything made of wood was brown; everything in fabric or cloth was red. Other than the one light bulb on the one lamp in the center of the room, there was no other color in the room. It was a creepy design nightmare, but probably a perfect setting for the mumbo-jumbo "reading" that I had agreed to.

The lamp sat on a round table, maybe 24-inches in diameter in the middle of the room. The table had a cloth covering, with dangling tassels around the edges. The chairs on opposite sides of one another flanked the table. They were big and bulky. Tall backs and heavily padded in soft cotton-like fabric. They were at one point probably high-end office chairs, but that one point was probably a century ago. Although they were comfortable, they were dated to say the least. And yes, they were both blood red.

"Hello, my name is Charles." Without standing, this skinny man with wire rimmed glasses probably in his 40s reached his hand out and shook mine. He was white skinned, almost oddly white, bordering albino. I couldn't make out his eye color, but they were dark. Very ominous looking. He had a thin layer of blond, straight hair parted to one side. I could see a tan tee-shirt under his dress shirt, under a denim vest. He had jeans on, and some kind of brown loafers. One might think he, too, was design nightmare, but somehow the mixture of materials looked like it all fit.

He asked a couple of questions to start. There was no small talk really, it was business immediately. The questions were nothing personal. Why was I here in the store? Who am I traveling with? Why was I traveling in New Orleans? Basic and polite type of questions. I answered each of them briefly and was shocked that he knew nothing about the Final Four playing in his own city, and couldn't tell me one team that was participating. He didn't seem very athletic, so I had a sense that he was telling the truth.

"What do you know of the Tarot?" Charles continued.

Walking into the back room just a few minutes prior, I had no clue what a reading was. My palms perhaps? Some crystal ball with Madam Olga gazing into my future? "Tarot?" I replied. "I dated a Tara once."

Charles pulled out a deck of cards and fanned them across the little table. There were maybe 25 or 30 cards in the deck. The cards were about the same size as regular playing cards. He explained that each card had a meaning, and the card would select me, but I had still to pick the card up and hand it to him to do the "reading." The Tarot cards he explained are used for divinatory purposes. I've been here for two minutes, and I'm already lost, bordering being uncomfortable.

I was given the card at the end of the reading. Charles reminded me that the card selected me. I still have it to this day. There is some lady on it in a frilly dress, sitting under a tree in a pasture with a moat in the background. There are birds in the air, and some old golden cup sitting on the grass beside her leg. The card never really touched me, after all it was just a thick piece of paper with a plastic covering. It had an odd-looking woman on one side and a hatched pattern on the other side, and that's it.

To be blunt, what did touch me was Charles. He had made a couple comments that bothered the crap out of me. I'm sure most of it was a trick or some technique used to elicit a response, but whatever he was doing worked. I wasn't freaked out, but he had my attention. He remained committed during my reading to discuss a presence in my life. Rather two human presences that were very active in my life. These presences he could "see" were females.

Years later, most of our conversation is just a blur. However, the comments and questions he had made about the "two women" in my life have always remained. At the time, we hadn't spoken of names, or what relation either had with me. He said that he could sense these women had impacts on my daily life. He continued that they were at the center of many decisions I make daily. As much as he tried to dig, we couldn't come up with what, or rather who he was "reading." Right before the conclusion of our talk, he looked me dead cold in the eyes and said, "Both of these women are departing from you within the next year." He couldn't elaborate any more and closed by saying, "That's all I have!"

I gave him $20, and I left that room that night and the city two days later questioning; actually still to this day, what he was able to "read"?

I've never had another reading since that trip back in 2003. I'm a Christian and don't play with the occult or any other of that kind of nonsense. Charles was kind and very polite. But something was off. I wouldn't fully appreciate his reading until later that same year.

In the fall of 2003, I lost my grandmother after a lengthy battle with COPD. She and I were very close. Later the same year, one week before Thanksgiving actually, my wife and I decided to end our marriage. We came up with a parenting plan that worked for everyone, and we chose to move forward in life as divorced parents. About 7 months or so since meeting Charles, two women who were in the center of my life were gone.

Gramps lived about 30 minutes or so from my home. When my wife and I separated, staying with him was a great option for everyone. He had the space, and I needed a place. I moved in the Monday prior to Thanksgiving, and it would be my first Thanksgiving without my kids. That sucked, but in perspective, it sucked for someone else a little more. My grandfather was also spending Thanksgiving without his bride, for the first time since World War II.

On the morning of Thanksgiving, we both felt off. Mentally, it just was weird. We had gone to bed the night prior without having any plans for Thanksgiving. We weren't going anywhere and hadn't planned on preparing a meal. We had each other and maybe some football to watch, but we both weren't feeling it. Roughly around 11 a.m., I had mentioned, or rather questioned, if perhaps maybe we should go to the hills to play some poker? Maybe we could grab something to eat in one of the nicer restaurants in the casino.

He looked at me and without uttering a word was up and out of his chair heading to his bedroom. I think we were both dressed and out the door in three minutes. He hadn't dressed or moved that fast in the last 20 years. Thinking back, that was comical and enlightening. Regardless of your age, enthusiasm rarely loses. The roads were wide open and by noon, we were sat for a Thanksgiving dinner together. The meal was perfect, and we didn't have to prepare or clean up afterwards.

By 1:30 or so, just after lunch, we were at two different tables playing cards. An hour or so later, we had managed to get on the same table, and then not too long afterwards had managed to sit by one another. We would sit there playing cards, talking, laughing, and winning for the next 12 hours. Neither of us got up except to go pee the rest of the day. We both had managed to do well against the other players at the table. What started off as an odd day, turned out to be something special. We pulled in the driveway at Gramps' house about 20 minutes after 3:00 a.m.

Black Friday, which many set aside for shopping, Gramps and I had other plans. We were back at it on the poker table. We had both gotten up at around noon that Friday. Thursday was so much fun, why not do it again? I sat in the living room fully dressed just watching TV. Gramps awoke and strolled down the hallway towards the living room and asked if I had any plans for the day.

"Gramps, my shoes are already on, and I waiting on you!" I said sarcastically and grinned at him with a slight smile.

"That's what I was hoping." We both chuckled. That was all he said as he turned around to get dressed himself. And just like the day prior, we were on the road, heading back to the casino only a few minutes later.

At the table where I was sat, was this guy named Abu Ross. That's only his nickname, but it's his real nickname. Anyway, this guy had immigrated to America many years prior from Jordan and after working some odd jobs here and there, he found the poker table was a better income source. It was my first time meeting the guy that Friday. It only took about an hour that day, but I quickly discovered what a solid card player he was. I'm not sure if I'd use the word professional, but he had an odd skillset. He knew when to bluff, and worse, he knew when you were bluffing. He was winning virtually every hand he was playing in.

At first it was frustrating. I could not beat the man. It didn't matter what I tried or how aggressive I tried to outplay him. Nothing worked. He was outplaying me and every other stiff at the table. During the process, he was stacking chips as fast as myself or others were throwing them in the pot.

To be honest, my first impression was he was just some random jackass having a good day. That was my first impression. Nobody plays this many hands and wins this many pots. I tried to dislike the guy, but he had a sense of humor and a type of sarcasm that I really appreciated. I began to admire the skillset and the way he conducted himself. About three hours into our session, I swear he raised my big blind (a forced bet in cards) in the dark.

It was my turn to act, and I hadn't looked at my cards yet. Everyone else before him had folded and he set a chip on his cards before declaring "raise!"

I know he didn't look, but he had a large stack of chips and was in a position to be a bully. The guy on the button and the other man in the small blind both folded. The action was on me. In poker playing against a big stack or bully, you must fold or raise them. That's the only way you can play. I looked down at my cards and had pocket Queens. Finally, I had something I could play back with ole' Abu Ross.

"I raise." I slid more money into the pot. The action was now back on him. Finally, he looked down at his cards. Muttering something under his breath I couldn't make out while he peeled his cards, he then made his words more obvious.

"It's about time you go to dinner with your grandfather, isn't it? I re-raise!" Abu slid more chips out. The pot was growing, and I couldn't wait to win this. The action was back on me, and I paused for a second after his comment thinking how in the world did this guy know about my grandfather? I hadn't played with this guy ever before, but I was about to be taught a few things that I still think about at times, even today. First, I hadn't said anything about Thanksgiving the day prior. I was confused and at awe with his comment. It would be sometime later, but I'd realize that Abu knew everyone in the building. He was a social man, who had fun with everyone, and more importantly, he paid attention to who was playing cards on his table, or another table across the room. That was lesson one, pay attention to your surroundings. It will help you with everything in life, including poker. The second thing was inexperience will always show its face. If you don't pay attention to both lessons, you can have so many things played "right," but end up going oh so bad.

"I re-raise." And flipped even more money into the pot. I looked directly at him trying to visually give the impression that his antics weren't going to work with me. At this point I'm still confident he's bluffing.

"I am going to re-raise and ask you kindly to go eat dinner with your grandfather." A slight pause before he continued. "Come on Donkey, save your money and go eat dinner." He smiled at me and mentioned, "You are beat!"

Abu started the hand bluffing, I'm certain of this. He made his first raise in the dark. The only two hands that are beating me pre-flop are a pair of Aces or a pair of Kings. The odds are 20 to 1 that he has neither. After his last raise, he had another $800 or so left in his stack. I was down to about $160. We traded a last round of raises and got my entire stack in the pot. After the rake, the pot had a little over $700 in it.

I proudly rolled over my Queens. To my dismay he rolled over Aces. Unbelievable! He started the raising marathon with a bluff, got caught, and was in the lead the entire time. The flop, turn and river ran out poorly for me. As Abu had suggested, it was time for dinner. Gramps was in a good spot to eat, and we both left our tables late afternoon. But I wasn't done with my new friend Abu just yet. He and I would clash again later that evening.

# 7

# Vail

*"We ought never to do wrong when people are looking."*
—Mark Twain

THE SHORT REALITY IS THAT GAMBLING is funny in that you'll spend a lot of time and money watering a plant that will never grow; a reality I wished I had learned many years ago. For our story here, I need to try and map out the when, where and how I got into this mess. Part of my dealing with my issues was looking back at some of the journey. Some parts of this story I can promise will be entertaining and worth the read. So, with that said, I wasn't done playing with my new friend Abu. Here we go.

Gramps wasn't ready to leave the casino after dinner. To be honest, neither was I. For the second day in a row, we ate like kings and laughed like jokers. Even though I had just gotten spanked by Abu, I still wanted to play. I had lost all the money won the day prior and now was playing on my own money again. Both of us got back into the game right after dinner. Again, we were at separate tables. Gramps was grabbing a seat at the 1-2 game, and they had an opening at a 2-5 game, and I took my seat (1-2 and 2-5 are blind sizes and two different tables).

The casino floor person walked me over to my new table. In the corner of the room, seat one on table 10. Unbelievably, the guy to my left, seat two, was no other than Abu. I had never played with the man before and now this was twice in the same day. We both chuckled at the oddity when we locked eyes. He had switched tables and just sent the guy in my new seat home. Just like me a couple hours ago, he sent him away confused and broke. Abu was roughly about $1,500 up in chips all stacked neatly in front of him. He was in a different mood though, a little edgy, kind of irritated. It was completely different than when I had left him and my money roughly two hours ago. Before I could ask what was up, I observed that he and another player at the table were having some words.

The two of them were arguing over a bad beat, bad run-out, poor play, one of those blah blah blah kinds of arguments. It appeared like a pointless conversation, but these are similar around most tables anywhere cards are being played. I've heard them before; I'll hear them again. The dealer tried to ease the two of them into a cease fire, but Abu and the other man kept at it. After a few other reckless comments, Abu muttered his final parting shot, "Have a nice day!"

I leaned over a whispered in Abu's ear, "What an asshole!"

Abu replied only loud enough for me, "You missed it. I guessed his cards, told him what I had, and then he still called me. He had a 2-outter (his opponent had to hit one of two remaining cards left in the deck to win the hand) and hit it. It only cost me $200, but then the genius has the audacity to tell me he out played me! Yea, what an asshole!"

Both of us kind of chuckled right then and ended up playing for the next six hours. We talked non-stop about poker, sports, friends and family. He continued to win pots, and I continued to struggle getting on track. I didn't care at this point. Poker to me has always been more about conversations and having fun while playing at the table. Winning money is only a bonus.

For the rest of the evening, when Abu and the "A-hole" were playing in a pot with one another, they at times did get a little chippy with one another. Wasn't a big deal, but you could feel the hostility between them the rest of the evening. A few times, they were raising each other with someone else in the pot. Their egos, a few times, had gotten in the way of good play and player X, (someone not involved with Abu's and A-Hole's battle) whoever that might be, just waited patiently and often drug in the pot. If anything, the battle was great entertainment.

"I don't care about the money. I'm going to wreck that guy's stack!" Abu mentioned quietly while winking in my direction.

The rest of the evening, we laughed non-stop while sharing our cards with one another seeing who could outplay the other players with a worse hand. We were raising when we shouldn't, playing hands that rarely win, bluffing where we could, and I was going broke. Oddly, Abu was still amassing chips.

Later in the evening, Abu asked a random question about being on the receiving end of a beat or an odd loss that I had witnessed or been through before we met. It was the kind of typical conversation that fellow poker players often speak of. Not necessarily as a point of gathering sympathy but rather getting a self-reassurance that you had played a particular hand well, even though the outcome wasn't in your favor. In poker it's called a bad beat.

Up until then, we had talked about his bad beat against the A-hole, and Abu's beat down on my stack hours earlier. Abu was being kind towards me, and I was enjoying our conversation. We were just breaking ground on our friendship, and I had mentioned that I had a story for him.

Not even a year ago I told him, while I was still married, I had prepared my wife for a game that I wanted to play in. A live one, and not in a casino. I didn't play that often, not much at all, but in the last couple years of our marriage, poker was exploding in popularity both live and online. My wife even started playing on her own account and that opened the door for me to play some cards here and there more regularly.

Anyway, there was a game in Vail, Colorado one Friday night. Roughly two hours or so from our house outside of Denver. It was a cash game, and the buy-in was $1,000. An old college buddy from the days at UNC tracked me down and asked if I still played cards. He contacted me roughly about a month prior to game night, and without hesitation, I told him I was in.

I continued the tale with Abu and told him that my wife would never in a million years be ok or permit me to use a $1,000 of our money to play a card game. If I was the defending world champion, the best player in the world, she would still say no. It would have been more like hell no. But I had committed, and I was going.

I had $600 +/- in my own online poker account that she was unaware of. I requested a check and had the money in roughly eight days. I also returned a couple things we had received for Christmas that year that we didn't need or care for and was oddly blessed with cash back as an option. The items were out of sight and out of mind. It was wrong, but I didn't tell her. Two weeks prior to the big game, I had randomly collected $800. The next two weeks I put together another $200 in odd ways, all legal but unethical as I wasn't sharing the details with my wife. Abu grinned at me and shook his head. He was a believer in Karma and knew where this story was heading. I continued.

About two nights before the big game, I said while at the dinner table my wife asked if I was still planning on going to the game? We hadn't really talked much about it the weeks prior as I was building my bank roll in private. "Of course I am," I told her. When she asked how much money I was planning on taking, I told her $200, maybe $300 dollars and that was it. She promptly replied that $200 she would feel comfortable with. What she didn't know was that the $200, plus my $1000 meant I'd have $1,200 to take. It was a little more than the $1,000 buy-in which gave me a little breathing room. As Friday approached, everything was set.

Abu and I kept playing cards and I kept telling him the story. On Friday morning, game day, I woke up to a decent snowstorm. It was snowing a little more than forecasted. I drove a 4x4 and didn't fear the drive to Vail that night. If the snow didn't taper off in the afternoon, I could leave work a tad early and make sure to get to the game for the 7 p.m. start, on time. That was the plan anyway.

Text messaging wasn't a big thing yet. It was kind of a pain in the ass. You had to push the 7 button on your cell phone 4 times to get the letter S to appear in a word with an S in it. Remember those days? Emails were big now, but land lines still ruled the communication world. My cell phone wasn't the electronic leash that it would soon become. At four in the afternoon, I was heading out in foot-deep snow into the mountains.

Abu commented a few times that he couldn't wait to hear where this was going as I kept re-calling the story. Of course, I continued and only paused if one of us was in a big hand. "Abu," I said, "that drive took me 5 hours. The traffic up the mountain got worse the farther I drove towards Vail. I had talked myself into believing that snowplows would have been working hard Friday night preparing for Saturday morning snow skiers. I guess the problem was when I started driving, it wasn't night yet. I didn't reach the condo in Vail until right before 9:00 p.m."

My first bad beat of the night was on that opposite side of the door. Abu listened intently and was chuckling at me as I was describing the train wreck unfolding. I knocked on the door twice before someone opened it. I got a little nervous that perhaps I was knocking on the wrong door, and late at that. I couldn't hear a thing. Normally a living room full of guys laughing, chatting, splashing the pot with plastic chips could be heard even from behind a closed door. I heard nothing.

After the second knock, I heard someone approaching the

door. Finally, I thought, as I was freezing my ass off. I'd find out right then, it was the correct door. The host opened the door and looked at me with amazement.

"Oh, my goodness dude. I sent an email at 4:00. We cancelled it because of the snow. I'm so sorry." I stood there in disbelief. I came in, used the bathroom and returned outside into the cold, blowing snow just minutes later. Abu asked if I checked my email before departing, I told him of course I had. About 3:45 that day. Turns out that was about 15 minutes prior to the cancelation email coming across.

At this point, Abu was rather enjoying himself laughing and ribbing me at my bad luck. "Rather bad beat," he corrected himself.

I corrected him. "Abu, the real bad beats were still yet to come!" He laughed a little more as I continued the story.

The drive back was nothing short of hell, I had told him. I pulled out of that condo complex maybe 10 minutes after nine and it took me eight hours to get home. The snow never stopped and not everyone on the road was driving in a 4x4. The road was dicey for me, miserable for several others along the way.

My average speed driving home was in the teens. I think I may have gotten to 30 miles per hour once. There were many times traffic came to a complete stop. The entire journey was a painful crawl all the way back home. I ended up driving just short of 13 hours total, and only ended up stopping for a pee break at the condo.

At last, just right before the sun came up, I finally pulled into the driveway at home Saturday around 5 a.m. Tired, cold, and a tad depressed, I quietly got in the house and made it to the pillow. I lay there and was thinking only how much I was looking forward to that game. What a waste.

At this point Abu and I were only playing big hands. My adventure tale had become the source of Abu's entertainment. I got his mind and poor play off the A-hole for a little bit. For some sick reason, often a poker player's bad beat is the source of others' entertainment. Abu was enjoying this. I'd pause for a brief second, looked Abu in the eyes and spoke, "One bad beat left!"

I probably dozed off around 5:30 a.m. My wife was up an hour or so later tending to the kids and getting the morning rolling for everyone except me. We hadn't exchanged words yet and she was ok with me sleeping until maybe noon, or so I thought. I was abruptly awakened with a smiling, cheery eyed wife sitting alongside me in bed. All I could think was something was up, I wasn't sure what was going on, but something was weird.

Abu had that look on his face like someone who was waiting for the coming punch line to a joke. He could sense something juicy was about to be revealed and said nothing in waiting. I added a little color to the story as I continued to speak. After all, it is a great story.

"Abu, she dug into my wallet!" He froze in silence waiting for me to finish.

I came in, tossed my keys and wallet on the kitchen counter. I had the $200 that I withdrew from our bank account and my $1,000 that I had massed together the prior month. It was all in there together, in the cash fold of my wallet.

"Oh my God, you did so good. I'm so happy for us," my wife gleefully mentioned as she rubbed my side.

"OH?" is all I could muster completely confused.

"I have a great idea, Hon," the wife continued. "Why don't we deposit $1,000 into our account and you can keep $200 in your wallet for another game soon? Call it your bankroll." She looked so proud to use the word bankroll.

Abu caught on about the same time I was finishing the ultimate bad beat story. It was his best and longest laugh of the night. I must have used the word idiot, and deservingly so at least five times in the past five minutes. My wife had found the $1,200, assumed that I had played and won that night, not knowing the hell I spent only driving and then suggested I start a bankroll with my winnings. *Funny,* I thought to myself laying there. *I lost $1,000 and never played a single hand!*

# 8

## Go F@%k Yourself.

*"I can teach you to jump up in five seconds-
it takes years to learn how to land properly."*
—David Lee Roth

ABU AND I CONTINUED PLAYING THAT NIGHT until the casino
closed at 2:00 a.m. Back then, the Colorado casinos closed daily
from 2:00 a.m. until 8 a.m. Super silly, and pointless, but that's
how government works. Most of the laws written and governed
in any state, or even the entire country, are written and managed
by persons that have zero business, ethical, or functional
reasoning behind the "laws" they've written. We all know that,
but I just wanted to rant a second. The 2:00 a.m. closing time is
a prime example. That's a political discussion for another day
perhaps. Back to Abu and me.

We both took turns attacking the A-hole Abu was at odds with
earlier in the evening. We were firing away at all comers with
good cards, crappy cards and everything in between. Winning
a pot was of course the goal, but just like those crazy games in
college, the entertainment behind the scenes was well worth
losing a few bucks here and there. At the end of the night, closing
time, Abu was up big. My stack, however? I was virtually broke,

but I had gained a few things. First, a friendship that to this day is strong as ever. Second, Abu introduced me to the phrase, "Have a nice day!"

Many of you might know perhaps or have heard of the phrase "See you next Tuesday." Well, if you were to break it down to alpha letters, C.U.N.T., you might know that it's a dirty insult. Whoever may have said that to you doesn't think highly of you. Trust me. It's widely popular overseas and amongst some in the crime world. I know what you might be thinking.

I was introduced to "Have a nice day" at a card table. Was the phrase something new to me? Like I had never heard it before? No, but hearing or even saying "Have a nice day" seems straight forward. Something of a kind gesture. What in the world could I be talking about? Well, let me explain.

Abu is from Jordan. He's a legal resident and has lived in the U.S. for quite some time. I've never been to Jordan, but I'm guessing from what I've been told and witnessed through Abu and his family here in the U.S., they and many alike from Jordan are very kind souls. Don't confuse that with being soft or weak, but people from that area of the world are at first proper and polite. That's their nature. They carry themselves with confidence and present a smile that is warming to everyone they come across. If you cross their paths poorly, they'll crush you. I've noticed all the ladies love that warm, amber skinned smile from any guy from that part of the world. When dealing with others, Abu and those alike have a belief system based on a kindness towards all of God's children. Telling someone to "Go F@&k yourself" wouldn't be something Abu's mother would think as positive or kind and would have never approved of such a statement.

Yup, you read that correctly. Playing cards that night with Abu for the first time I learned that he has a favorite phrase, or rather a most liked one liner that at times has a perfect place in a conversation. We spoke and laughed for hours about it after he told me the secret meaning of the phrase. "Have a nice day," presented with a charming smile doesn't always mean what you think it might mean.

We were racking up chips at 2:00 a.m., preparing to head for the door for the evening. They would always deal the last hand at a minute before 2. Many players at the table had been there for hours on end. Some players all day up until closing. A couple of friends playing with some strangers, it had been a mixed table of personalities. Then of course was the A-hole that never seemed to change his demeanor. He was rude, nasty and sarcastic the entire night. When you won a hand against him, you heard about it. When he ran you down with an inferior hand, you really heard about. He was also chiming in on hands when he wasn't even in the pot. A big no-no in poker. So, when hands were shaking and good-byes were being exchanged at the end of the night, Abu made is parting shot very clear with the A-hole. "Have a nice day sir!" Translated.... "Go F@&K Yourself!"

I met up with Gramps at the casino valet 20 minutes later. He'd gone bust on the poker table where he was playing and went downstairs and started feeding the video poker machines with twenty-dollar bills. I'm not sure how he did it, but we joked about it all the way back to his house. He had said after he was done playing live cards, and getting beat up, he proceeded to the video version and couldn't lose. Bouncing around a couple different machines, he took $400 off one, $500 off another and close to closing time, hit the last machine for $1,200.

I had Gramps back home a little after 3:00 a.m. and he was done. Not just for the night, but the entire weekend. He was beaten. Sometime before sunrise I finally fell asleep and dozed off missing the card room. I had grinded hard for two days, went on some runs of both good and bad luck. I wasn't planning on playing again the next day as I had been at it hard for a couple days in a row and needed a break. My phone laying on the table next to my bed rang a few minutes before 8:00 a.m.

When the phone rings on a Sunday morning before 8 a.m., it's normally something really good, or something really bad. I rolled over and grabbed the phone and the number I didn't recognize. I didn't answer the call. After about a minute, my phone would beep if someone left a message. It did, and I listened to a message from Abu. "Call me." It was short, direct and his voice sounded intriguing, almost like he was up to something. If you knew Abu today, you would know the voice and know that he is normally up to something. LOL.

Anyway, I did call back a few minutes later and right to business, Abu hit me with it.

"I want you to come to a private game tonight. Bring $2,000 maybe $3,000 and you should plan on being there until Tuesday."

He said that last part joking, but he really wasn't. Some of these home games could last for days on end. I've witnessed over the last several years, guys who worked all day, came and played at 7:00 p.m., play all night, and head to work in the same clothes from the day before having not slept a minute. That would be an amazing enough part of any story if it wasn't for the fact that in this one game we had a person having worked two days at his normal job with a card game in between shifts, and made it back to the same game, following the next work shift. I wasn't there for it all, but I was told between work and poker he made it almost three full days, barely eating, not sleeping and wasn't a minute late to his VP role at a BANK!

Back to my phone call with Abu. I advised him I'd love to come but only had maybe 500 bucks. He chuckled and said he'd spot me $1,500, but the buy-in was a minimum $2,000 and most guys would have that and several re-buys ready. As a side note, I met the guy just days earlier and he's now loaning me money to play? That's the kind of guy he is. The game was No-limit Hold'em and some of the guys playing that night lost $2,000 every 30 minutes or so. They loved getting together with the guys, having some laughs and losing $10,000 a night wasn't a big deal. They loved action and at the time Colorado was a limit state so playing in the casinos wasn't an option for large bet players. If you've played No-limit, you understand the rush.

Abu mentioned on the phone that he thought my style of play and personality would lend to some healthy paydays perhaps, and him getting me involved with this kind of game would be good for both of us. Did I mention for getting into the game, I was on the hook for 5% of my winnings for the first year of play. It was a weekly game, and it often ran even two full tables. On any given Sunday night, there was always over $100,000 in cash in that house.

I did make that game, got my loan and took a seat. The action was fast and as promised, it was heavy. Meaning even though we were playing 5-10 (blinds) you would rarely see a pot for less than several hundred if not a few thousand, and that was often. The first hand I played about 30 minutes after sitting down was Jack King of Diamonds. Pre-flop it was $80 to call, and we had 4 total callers. The pot was $240 pre-flop. The flop was JJ6. I flopped trip jacks and was terrified. The action was checked to me, and I checked. Thinking back, I'm not sure if I checked to trap or checked because I was terrified to have to bet probably all my stack. The turn was no help, and the first position player bet $200. The other two behind me folded and now the river was heads up with me last to act. The river was another blank and he fired out $500. I was terrified. One hand in, almost my entire starting stack was being committed to the pot. I had trip Jacks with a King kicker. These days I would have my entire stack in that pot so fast, but back then, my first brush with a game that big I wanted to go home and call my mommy. I won that pot, and the first thing Abu does is grill me for not raising the river. He wasn't wrong, but as I mentioned, I was a wreck mentally, being hand number one of the night.

I ended up playing until about 4 a.m. I had a little over $3,600 in front of me. Not bad for my first night in that big game. Several guys had over $10k in front of them. A few lost that easily. After paying Abu the $1,500 plus the running fee of 5%, I was walking with over a thousand bucks. I have a reason for sharing this part of the story with you, and it's not about a thousand bucks.

If you have ever sat at a poker table, you'd agree that the conversations are wide open. Discussing politics and religion is kinda taboo, but everything else is open season. I only knew one guy in the room so for me to joke about some guy's wife or call his kids fat and ugly wasn't going to happen. Others though, friends or regulars that knew each other provided a night full of some crazy and other times hilarious commentary. I just sat back most of the night and laughed.

In the room that night was an older gentleman, let's call him Barry, that at one point when the conversation took a serious twist, added something I never will forget. I wasn't in trouble with my sports betting yet, but his words, rather the mix of his words coupled with the look on his face have always bothered me. I knew nothing of the man he was speaking of but sitting there and piecing together the story being spoken between a few players and Barry, I knew something bad had happened.

The short version was that someone, I think his name was Francois, maybe Frankie, owed a debt. Some kind of loan or gambling debt, I'm not too sure. Barry played well, and I swear he won every pot he was in. He laughed very little, and he didn't bother himself with most of the chatter being tossed around the room all night. All he seemed to do was stack chips anytime he was in a pot. When the conversation about a debt came up, another gentleman at the table looked towards Barry and asked if Francois had ever settled. I had no idea and still don't know who Francois was.

The room went silent. Barry exhaled, viewed the player who just asked the question and responded looking from over the thick black rims of his glasses perched atop his nose and said, "We got our money."

Another minute of silence before Barry was asked another

question. The vibe in the room had taken an ugly, almost scary turn. I knew nothing about anything, and I was even nervous to hear that response. After another brief bit of silence, it was another player at the table who seemed to know the back story or perhaps something about Barry that asked, "How'd you get it?"

Having gone through what I would deal with years later, I should have paid attention to the coming warning being verbalized that night. Would you call it a premonition or forecasting perhaps? I'm not sure, but to this day, his response still bothers the crap out of me.

Barry looked towards the man who just asked how he got the money, and with an almost cocky demeanor, he responds in a frightening tone, "We got it the hard way."

There weren't five words said over the next couple of hands. Again, the room being eerie for a while might be an understatement. I knew nothing about Francois, Barry or any debts, but a few guys around the table knew something bad had happened and the subject should probably not be talked about anymore, and it wasn't. As luck would have it, the next pot I played was against Barry and I can't remember what I had, but I almost guarantee I had him beat and I still laid down (folded) a solid hand. Just in case he wanted to collect "the hard way."

# 9

# Happy Ending

*"If you even dream of beating me,*
*you'd better wake up and apologize."*
—Muhammad Ali

Treasure Island is a hotel and casino on the famous Las Vegas strip. They changed the name to TI several years ago for some ridiculous reason but that building owns one of the craziest gambling stories I ever read about. I don't remember his exact name or when it actually happened, but I think I have most of the other details correct. Some of the exact information is not important, but this man's journey is my all-time favorite.

Let's call our gambler for this story Dean. Why do you ask? Well, I've only known one guy named Dean and he was a real dumbass, so the name fits. You'll soon find out why. The story started off noting Dean had lost his job and went home to figure out the next play in life. The story continued that things didn't improve at home that morning and he left soon after a fallout with his wife. When he left home, he had nothing packed; he only had his severance check in hand.

For some reason, unknown to most, he chose Treasure Island as the place. It was there that he walked in and went straight to the cashier to cash his last payroll check. I don't remember the total, but less than $400 comes to mind. He didn't have a room, no plans to eat, hadn't mentioned needing to see anyone, he was just there to gamble a tad. Now the story I read went into a little more of the exact details, but again, that's not important for this story here. The last paragraph or two of what I read in the article still blows my mind to this day. At the conclusion of his little adventure, Steve Wynn, the owner at the time of Treasure Island, personally walked Dean to the door, thanked him for his business, opened the door to a casino-provided limousine and wished him well on his way to wherever he wanted to go.

That was of course after almost two full weeks of a complimentary stay. The property took care of the room, meals, drinks, the spa, and even threw in some gifts for our guy Dean. Not bad for a guy who had less than $400 on him when he sat down to play blackjack that first afternoon. Of course, you probably need to know in those ten plus days, at one point Dean was up over $2.3 million in winnings. When Mr. Wynn walked him out, he had less than $100 to his name.

I mention that story because I've been asked a few times why I think I've done what I've done. Perhaps while reading this, you can think of someone you know or whom you've read about that has done the same similarly crazy things. Trust me; the stories are out there, many of them. Why would anyone, or the countless other Deans out there, me included, make such poor decisions? When you beat someone, or say a casino, for "X" amount of money, why not just leave? Take your money, count your blessings and just GO! The easy answer to most of those questions looks simply like nothing but greed. Dean and others alike are greedy, and a few extra bucks just aren't enough. Many won't know this, but for gamblers, especially poker players, there's more to winning money going on.

As America's growing acceptance for gambling seems to be expanding daily, I've run across several articles in the last several years that have been titled, "Why Gambler's Gamble." Although some articles are entertaining, I struggled at times to completely agree with any one of them. One writes about escapism and our need as humans to unwind, relax, maybe avoid or just escape. I can see maybe a little of that. Another wrote about our need as individuals to find glitz or glamour in our attention-starved lives, perhaps. There is of course the social aspect and its allure that I relate to. I like nothing more than talking and getting to know people. Of course, some articles tapped into our need as humans to seek adventure or take risk. I'd also agree with aspects of those studies. Some of the articles I did like, but most missed the point. You can always tell when someone writes from experience or opinion.

Maybe it's from my own journey perhaps. I've also picked up or witnessed and shared similar journeys with other gamblers. You would be amazed at what some people have done or are doing. But my answer for why gamblers gamble is pretty simple. It's not scientific to say, but I've run across the same thing in almost each and every case that I've explored, and that includes my journey. I believe there is a primary reason why I and other Deans out there do what we do. We like to compete; we like to win. Let me explain.

I'd preface that statement with the need to win is what I've seen with poker players primarily. I think it can also be said about players of other table games to some degree, but not as much with slot players or other games of chance. Poker players are a little different breed.

Texas Dolly, his nickname, was an absolute legend in the poker world. Before finding his way to the poker felt, he was one heck of an athlete. He was almost at a professional level in sports before injuries sidelined that career. Even with various physical issues, anything he did outside the poker room was often something in competition. I could write an entire book about former and current athletes that have found a poker table as well. And it's not just athletes either. World-class chess and backgammon players have often found the poker table. Business tycoons and professionals in just about every trade imaginable have all hit or regularly play poker. In 2017, a Hollywood major motion picture named *Molly's Game* dove into the world of high stakes poker and the variety of players from around the world who played in that nosebleed game. If someone tells me this is just for money, I say BS.

All these instances and experiences aren't the same. But there are a couple identifiers that are unique and common to each. Poker offers something that so many other interests in our lives can't compete with. Pick a sport, any sport. Say golf as a for instance. I love that game and for years have tried to improve it without success. My handicap is stuck, and I've resigned to the fact that playing on the seniors' tour probably isn't going to happen. However, I have faced off with a few professional golfers and we've traded shots on the poker felt. In what other profession can you find where the competition isn't better balanced, giving everyone a shot to win? And there lies the gambler's issue, rather desire, to win!

At any early age, just about everyone I knew spent some time competing in something. Perhaps it was little league football for me or soccer for you. As we grew up, maybe we had a common friend who excelled in studies and was on the debate team. That same kid was also a spelling bee champion years before. His sister played classical piano, and every year Mom and Dad had her competing against other youths for whatever that might have looked like. Today, me and the spelling bee champion still have the want, need, and desire to compete and win. What poker offers is a chance for anyone to be a champion, and oh yeah, maybe win a few bucks.

Another famous Hollywood movie titled *Rounders* specifically followed a couple of guys and their hobby/job adventure in the world of poker. There is a scene buried towards the end where our star of the show was playing an actual legend in the poker world. The scene goes on just briefly about the game and high stakes but the story line for this particular scene was about the movie's main character just wanting to beat the superstar, just win or outplay the man. That same story doesn't work being told with me beating Tiger Woods on the golf course. It's not realistic; it's not the same, it would never happen, even in Hollywood. But on the poker table, let's go Tiger!

Some of those articles I mentioned earlier that were missing something, is the internal drive or desire to compete, or win that most humans have. I'll argue all day about this, but you can find that drive in just about everything we do in life. Even in my regular day job, I'm sure like yours, our bosses are wanting results, expecting performance today that is better than yesterday, and each of them are hoping we are getting results. Translated; just like the great, late Al Davis of the Oakland Raiders, "Just win, Baby!"

The pressure and desire share the same destiny. I don't care what it is, golf, bowling, ping pong, or in my case, poker. Oddly, as much as I enjoy some non-competitive hobbies, I'll probably always have a need to beat your ass. I'm not alone and you know it. I was recently playing poker in a senior center in Florida with a bunch of blue-haired old ladies that didn't care about the money. Half of them probably were sitting on small fortunes in their personal lives, but at that penny ante game, each one of them was gunning for me. Even though making friends and having something social to-do is important, they played their butts off and why? They wanted to win! That desire carries off into sports betting. Want proof, go make a $5 bet on your favorite team and watch what happens. It may only be $5, but collecting from the house is still a win, and nothing is better than winning.

Now I was far from having my issues even close to cleaned up, but this is a time in life around that Super Bowl disaster, for maybe the first time where I can remember stopping to reflect on things. Literally, like get up in the morning and journal or have longs talks in the mirror. Personal, professional, financial, all of it and everything that goes with it. I wasn't trying to be a wrecking ball, nor was I wanting to have anyone get wrecked along the way, but I was dancing with trouble that soon I'd see another ugly side of.

# 10

# Hard Rock

*"When you have a lot of money,*
*it's easy to do the right thing."*
—Benny Binion

MOST READING THIS HAVE PROBABLY HEARD the name Benny Binion, (real name). He's long passed away, but those that knew of him credit Benny for the World Series of Poker. It was at his hotel in downtown Las Vegas in 1970 where the world-famous event started prior to moving to Caesar's Entertainment where it runs annually today. This one-time gangster style criminal operated the Horseshoe Casino downtown and besides the credit for starting the WSOP, he was also known to be one of the only properties in the world that would take whatever size bet you wanted to make. One of his longtime friends once said, if you could set the bet on a gaming table or park it outside, Benny would take your action. To say he knew and loved gamblers was an understatement.

I believe Benny and I would have liked each other personally, and I would have loved to have met the man. His stories about some gamblers are legendary. I've wondered if a guy like him would have steered me differently if I could have asked for his advice prior to making what would soon be the largest bet of my life. I'd like to think he would have encouraged me to go for it.

I believe it was 1:00 in the afternoon on Super Bowl Sunday before anyone from our group found me. The night before Super Bowl Sunday just happened to be my birthday, February 1st. Being in Vegas for the Super Bowl, having the Broncos playing as the favorite and celebrating my birthday was almost more fun than any one guy should deserve. Anyway, it was a few hours to kick-off, and I was playing poker trying to just relax and drink as much water as I could into my dehydrated body. Do I need to remind you the night prior was a Saturday, and we were all in Vegas? Oh, was I a happy man, but hurting that Sunday morning.

We were all staying at the Mandalay Bay and Ford (his real name will remain a mystery, but he likes Ford trucks) found me in the poker room that Sunday afternoon. This part of the story is significant, and it will add some flavor, so hold on. It may help you, the reader, understand a few things about me and what I was about to do that would drastically alter my life and give us all the story you are reading currently. I'll add this as a quick side bar, the amount of money our group spent gambling on that Saturday can be best summed up in one word. Gross. But the worst was still yet to come.

Ford had come to find me to get help with something. He had gone through all his play money the night before and was attempting to pull money off a credit card. Understand this, Ford was and still is a very successful businessman and needed some funds off one of his high limit credit cards. I think it was an American Express Black which carries no limit. The kind of money he needed wasn't something you get from the ATM. Ford isn't much of a gambler but as they say, "when in Rome," so he was playing the weekend to his limits which were a tad higher than most of ours, and he needed some more cash. Like A LOT more.

He came to me for help as I probably stood out amongst our

group as a guy who knows how the system works. The how, when, and where to get money the best way possible. I jumped up from the card table and walked him through the process of going straight to the cashier and working on the casino on a reduced or zero fee cost for the withdrawal that higher stakes players get when pulling out large sums of money. They won't just offer it to a regular player, and I wasn't about to let him pay the high fees if I could help it. Most casinos do this for big known players, but not just average Joes off the street. I mean God forbid if the big player must pay a withdrawal fee like the rest of us degenerate gamblers. Anyway, I know how the system works; thus the reason Ford probably came to find me when he needed some cash.

We didn't have the cash for long either, like maybe an hour. Something else Ford wasn't familiar with was betting prop bets on the Super Bowl. I could be wrong, but I think he mentioned right there that he had never placed a sports bet before and that day, the Super Bowl would be his first time taking action. To be honest, I felt kinda cool and privileged to be escorting my pal with a small brick of hundred-dollar bills to the sports book area to place bets at that money level. Ford trusted me, and off we went. I couldn't care less about the poker game I was playing at the time and just left my chips there.

Las Vegas has a few days each year that are considered the most important days in the casino business. On New Year's Eve for one, you can't get a room in town due to the amount of people partying and celebrating. For most guests, there is probably some gambling, too. March Madness (basketball) is another draw that packs the casinos and of course they have a variety of yearly trade shows that bring in guests and of course, gamblers alike. However, nothing generates money in the sports book like the volume that the Super Bowl brings in.

I say this and need to include that if you sports bet you know what a "prop" bet is. And if you know what a prop bet is, you may have witnessed or experienced the next tidbit of information about betting on Super Bowl Sunday. The line starts Friday afternoon that weekend in just about every casino with a sports book. It gets really long about Saturday afternoon and by the time the late betters hit the casino floor, that same line is one of those you hear about that wraps about the sports book, down the hall, around the corner and out the door. No lie, I've heard of guys waiting for 2 hours to place a $20 bet on Super Bowl Sunday just to be "in the game." Well Ford had a little line to deal with and a lot more than $20 we were planning on wagering.

For those who don't know what a prop bet is, it's a particular bet on some aspect of the game. Will the star quarterback throw for over or under 300 yards? You do your homework, make a guess, or even flip a coin and place a bet on what you think the outcome might be. Speaking of flipping a coin, yes, you can bet heads or tails in the Super Bowl on the coin toss. That, my friend, is a prop bet. And they have hundreds of different bets you can make on the game. You can even bet on the color of the Gatorade thrown on the winning coach. If gambling was a circus, the Super Bowl would be the Ring Master.

Typically, while you're in line, you dig through these little magazines with all the different prop bets listed that you could place. They all have a 4-digit code for ease of betting. You go to the counter say something like "I'd like to bet $20 on bet number 0314 and while you're at, give me another $20 on bet number 1123. It's that simple and should be fairly fast. Eight or 10 cashiers can dust through a line of a couple hundred bettors in no time on any regular day. On Super Bowl Sunday, with thousands of gamblers, it takes a while longer.

So, Ford and I were digging through what he wanted to bet on waiting our turn, moving up in line slowly but surely. One bet Ford liked was Denver would win by a point total of 14 points or more. Denver on average beat their opponents that same year in the regular season by two touchdowns so why not in the big game? A two-touchdown victory which is a long shot, paid 7 to 1. Meaning a dollar bet on that prop bet would net you a $7 win. Ford had no plans of betting a dollar on that bet or any other bet.

After about 45 minutes or so, we finally got to one of the cashiers at the sports book. Still digging through our prop bet guidebook and not 100% settled on where all what money is going, the cashier blurts out, "Fellas, you should have your minds made up, this isn't tough, let's go!" His tone was nasty and before we could even respond or make a bet, he blurted out something else rude. He had been dealing with $20 dollar bettors all day and probably was tired of explaining "how this worked" to everyone in line, but his attitude was piss poor.

Just before the time the third comment came, Ford did the most awesome thing I'd seen all weekend. He could have responded with something rude or tossed some hostility back at the cashier, but rather as cool as James Bond, he looked him square in the eyes and made only a slow, calculated single motion with his hand. Ford reached down and brought from below the counter his stack of hundred-dollar bills bound together in stacks of $5,000 each. Those stacks, those were multiple stacks by the way. Not a single word was needed but he still looked at the cashier as if almost to say *shut up and let me think*. The cashier responded politely, "Fellas I apologize. Take your time."

Ford ended up in total with about 15 random prop bets. I think his small bet was $500. His large bet was $10,000 on Denver to win outright. I was nervous for him walking around with that kind of cash an hour before we just slid it back across another counter at the sports book. With all the prop bets he had made, some real long shots, he had potentially tens of thousands in could-be winning tickets if Denver won the game. He was set, and we both were looking forward to kickoff.

It was roughly 2:30, a couple hours before kickoff, and the rest of our group was starting to assemble on the casino floor for our attack on the Hard Rock Hotel Casino. It was off the strip, and a property where the owner of my company, BJ, had done a major renovation in a restaurant called Culinary Dropout. We had VIP service and table number 1 under the big screen in the dining room. The management had turned the entire place into a Super Bowl party, and it was packed with Broncos and Seahawks fans alike. The energy is what you expect in Vegas, and everyone was on cloud 9.

We grabbed our table; we started ordering drinks and discussing who bet what and for how much. Our table was all guys, a tad cocky and fully confident that the Broncos were hours away from a World Championship. Everyone marveled at Ford's big $10,000 bet and we made fun of a few other guy's little, safe, sissy bets. One guy from our group got so much ribbing he up and left the table to run over to the sports book and place a man's-sized wager.

During the pre-game mess at our table unfolding, nobody had seemed to notice that I hadn't said a word about my action. Not one person asked what I had bet and for how much. With less than an hour until kickoff, I was still pondering how much of my $4,800 in my virtual account I was going to place in action. Everyone in our group had visited the sports book and had made their bets. Each guy in our group made all kinds of prop bets, 100% of them on the Broncos. I hadn't made a single bet yet.

Part of my thought process was that our legendary QB in Denver had one little strike on his almost perfect resume. Many had said, especially sports bettors and bookies alike, that the man just couldn't play, or at least struggled in cold weather games. The bulk of his career was spent in the Dome of Indianapolis. Super Bowl Sunday for some dumb-ass reason was being played in New York that year. That little detail did make me second guess betting my entire $4,800 on this single game.

One thought I had was to just bet $3,000, maybe $4,000 and pocket the rest of my funds from my online account. Maybe a straight up money line bet, which would be the safest. In my heart, I was confident that this game was already over, and it was yet to even start. The Seahawks and their young QB were nothing that scared me. Their Legion of Doom, or Boom, or Dumb, whatever they hell they called themselves was filled with a bunch of ego maniacs, who talked a big game. The more I heard any of them speak the more I laughed and thought this might be the easiest money ever. I wanted, rather needed, to wait to see what the line was doing. What did the last-minute gamblers think, and which way was the betting world leaning.

I sat there laughing, listening to my buddies playfully fight about nothing while drinking beer and eating cheesy pretzel bits. It was such a good feeling, so much fun, such a happy time. We were all waiting for kickoff which now was about 20 minutes away.

Now bookies don't take verbal bets. In that arena, you must jump online or do it with a text message. Some kind of paper trail was required. I stepped away from the table with my smart phone and sent the text. I had made up my mind on the bet. Denver scored a record number of points that year. They scored 50+ three times. They had arguably the best QB to ever play the game. The team's VP was another former all-world QB who had won a couple of his own championships. Could Seattle really beat the Broncos? No way in HELL!

I wanted to take full advantage of the moment and capture as much money as possible. I was, after all, in Vegas and that's what you do. Gamble in hopes of winning more money. In this case, I decided at the last minute, rather midway texting my bet to LT, to do it all. All weekend I wrestled and considered only betting only a part of the money in my account, but really why? I was here to make money. A parlay bet would pay the best. Finally, just a few minutes before kickoff I texted in my bet. "Two Team parlay; Denver to cover and the over. $5,000!"

# 11

# Living in Denial

*"Be at war with your vice, at peace with your neighbors, and let every year find you a better man."*
—Ben Franklin

THERE IS A CLASSIC MOVIE from the 1980s that stars Robert De Niro and Charles Grodin. It's called *Midnight Run,* and if you have seen the movie, you might recognize what I'm about to tell you. If you haven't seen the movie, there is a great scene that takes place on a train during the two characters' adventure together. It's a fun movie. You can find this clip online under "Living in Denial" on YouTube.

During the scene, De Niro's character is eating dinner and Grodin's character is questioning De Niro's behavior, specifically on what he is eating. Rather, Grodin is eloquently trying to assault his captor verbally. He does this throughout the entire movie, most often very humorously. Anyway, De Niro in this same scene has the rare opportunity to flip the script on Grodin about something completely different using the same exact line of questioning that was just presented to him. "You are aware of your behavior, yet you continue to do things that aren't good for you? That sounds kind of foolish don't you think?" You might need to watch it to fully understand and appreciate the scene, but it's a classic. I didn't know it then, but while walking back to the table in the Hard Rock, I was about to be presented a rather foolish opportunity for myself.

Before I got back to the table, my cell phone began to ring off the hook. A couple of other friends, my brother, and LT himself had called 4 times in just about 2 minutes. I was in a loud casino and was just about back to our table in the restaurant when I noticed that I had also received back-to-back missed texts from LT. I didn't answer any of the calls or even read the text at first. I would have had to step outside, like as in outside the building to talk with LT and really, I wasn't in the mood. Why, might you ask?

Because bookies just never get enough money. They are the best salesmen in the world and their business is to extract money. This was part of the deal when gambling with a bookie. A casino just asks you what you would like to bet and that's the end of it. You leave the counter and go away. A bookie though? They never stop. His team did quite well. Say you bet $400, they will call you back to "confirm" the bet and you hear this. "While I have you on the phone, why not also put down another $100 on XYZ to happen. Or what about we at least round this one bet off to $500?" It was the game most all good bookies played. All it took was just one phone call, and before you knew it, you'd agreed somehow to double your bets. I had made my $5,000 bet, was looking forward to the payday, now it was time to rejoin my friends and watch the Broncos beat up the piss-poor Seahawks.

I was back at the table and ready for the game. It was about 5 minutes before kickoff I noticed another 2 missed calls and a handful of 911 texts from LT. This wasn't normal for him, something was up. His last text read something like "Call me, 911, NO BET!" I froze for a brief second and was good with no bet. I thought if he didn't want my money, to hell with him, I'll just take my winnings from the playoffs that I had already banked and that will be it. That was my first thought and that was only for a brief second before curiosity got the better of me. Why no bet? Looking back, how unfortunate I was not making a fortunate decision and only compounded things by hustling outside the room to make a quick call. If only I hadn't flipped my phone over, this story would have never come to be.

The following is a very quick re-cap of a quick conversation between LT and I after I finally did end up calling him back. We were only minutes from kickoff. "Shawn, you have been a good guy and always pay. I enjoy you as a friend and doing business with you, but this amount is WAY over your book rate (rate of action bet per week and the caped amount allowed to bet week in and week out). I'll book this bet, but you need to re-confirm and understand this very clearly. Pay day, one way or another is Tuesday. Are we clear on this?"

My response back was curt and quick. "What are you talking about? I have $4,800 in my virtual account on your site. You aren't going to take my bet for another $200?" As I was talking, the entire thing was just weird, something was off. It was roughly 2 minutes before kickoff before he hit me with it.

"Shawn, read your text again. "Two Team parlay; Denver to cover and the over. $50,000!" I'll take the bet, but you need to re-confirm in the next minute or NO BET! Good luck."

He hung up and I was literally on the clock. My $5,000 bet was going to pay $13,000. The $50,000 bet would pay over $130,000. I looked back at the message, and he was correct. I had texted him a bet accidentally of $50,000. My normal weekly book limit was $3,000. I could never get in serious trouble at $3,000 per week. I was up from the playoffs and the $5,000 in my account meant the bet was almost a free bet. In most cases with anything in life, a zero, or in this case an extra zero would mean nothing. This would be different. A $50,000 bet I could NOT cover. I didn't have the resources, and in the slightest chance I was of losing this bet, the next morning, Monday, life would be much different.

As I walked back into the casino heading to the table, I glanced at a TV and our legendary QB, helmet on and looking ever so confident, had all the attention on him. The entire country, down to the camera man knew the Broncos were only a couple hours away from winning Super Bowl 48. I stopped just outside the restaurant; both teams were on the field for kickoff, and I re-confirmed my bet order. You are damn right tomorrow morning was going to be different, like in $130,000 different, I said to myself. I re-sent in my bet, confirming everything. "Two Team parlay; Denver to cover and the over for $50,000. Go Broncos!"

I sat down next to Ford at the table and grabbed the first cocktail in front of me. I'm not sure if it was even mine, but I needed a drink. As excited as I was for the game, it was now an entirely different level of excitement after doing what I had just done. Perhaps it was nausea, I felt good but not right. Another movie scene popped into my head was from another 80s classic called *Bachelor Party*. One of the bachelor's best friends was out on the town rounding up strippers for the groom's bachelor party. He meets a pimp in a shady part of town who agrees to various terms and offers a little threat to the would-be-groom's best friend if he doesn't live up to the terms. After hearing the terms, most of which were out of the best friend's control, he turns around and walks off in disbelief pondering aloud to himself. "I just bet my balls and shook on it!"

Denver received the opening kickoff, and the Broncos QB with the rest of the offense trotted out on the field. The energy in the entire building was buzzing like we were live in New York at the game ourselves. Seahawks fans were here and there, but Broncos fans were everywhere. It was in Las Vegas, the gambling capital of the world and anyone that was betting pretty much was betting on the Broncos. The entire world sat waiting, anticipating what the first play would be. Toss right, maybe a run up the middle or probably a deep pass on the outside just like we had done so many times all year long. Nope, not even close. A fluke miss-snap, right over the QB's head and into the end zone for a quick 2-point safety 8 seconds into the game. "Are you F@&King kidding me?" I yelled out.

I wish that was the end of the nightmare. Literally the only enjoyment of the entire game was the opening kickoff. The Broncos were tied then, and they still had a chance at that point. The Super Bowl each year is typically the highest rated show on television each year. This year probably even more so due to the love affair that everyone had with our legendary QB. Pretty much the entire planet was watching this train wreck unfold play after play. Hats off to the Seahawks and their fans as they crushed Denver. The only thing I had correct with my bet, was the over. Denver lost 48-8 in a gross football game, and I had just lost $50,000. I only blurted, "are you F@&King kidding me," no less than 10 times over the past few hours. This might be the right time to mention I was a little short on that $50k bet. Actually, I was very short. If you knew me personally, you might even say I was short the whole way.

The mood in Vegas was different after the game. Not just amongst our group, but the entire town was a little off. The energy was dead, and nobody had planned on wrapping up the weekend like with what had just happened. Some of our guys went to a club. A few others went to dinner, and a few just went to bed. Me and another guy or two walked around to a few casinos and did nothing. We ended up back up at our hotel and I played a little craps. After all, perhaps I could turn my last $300 into $50,000, it happens all the time. Said no man ever.

At roughly 5 a.m., a few of us who never made it to bed met the others and we all headed for the airport. We had to work that morning once we landed back in Denver. At this point I hadn't told a single soul. I was saving this story for after the game. A celebration kind of a victory perhaps; but in defeat, I didn't want to admit this to anyone. We landed, I went to work and that was the day. I never heard a word from LT. As I went to bed finally about 8 that night, all I could think for and pray about was that somehow, someway I missed the bet and it wasn't booked. It was never booked with LT perhaps. God does perform miracles and perhaps I was in the middle of one. I dozed off with a tad bit of hope.

That all changed Tuesday morning.

# 12

# Bet with Someone Mean

*"Everything is funny as long as
it is happening to somebody else."*
—Will Rogers

TUESDAY MORNING, THE DAY AFTER, I was up at 5 a.m. (typical) and there was a text on my phone from LT. I received it over the night while asleep. It's what I had feared, and it was short and to the point. It read, "Bummer Shawn. I emailed you the payoff and bank schedule. Please confirm you have received this and save your deposit receipts."

I'm sure many of you reading this have at some point in your life attended some rah-rah speech by some well-known public speaker. I have many times, and I love them. Maybe the presentation you attended was on improving your professional life or getting more satisfaction on some personal matters. Perhaps someone like Tony Robbins was the main attraction or even Gary Vaynerchuk? My personal favorites are Les Brown, Jack Canfield, and a hidden gem, Hal Becker. Regardless of whom you've listened to or why you were there in the first place, I'd bet you found some kind of motivation following the presentation.

I have had my favorite speakers over the years, but the most influential person in my life might be a little different than what you think. Who is yours? I ask that because I didn't know how to answer that way back when, but I can answer that differently, today. The absolute greatest motivational person you will ever do business with is someone that you make a bet with who, to be blunt, is an asshole. Better yet, want to get more disciplined and really change some aspects of your life? Make a wager with someone mean. Someone who might actually harm you personally or professionally, perhaps someone who may do both.

When I woke up that Tuesday morning, and read that text to say it ruined my day would be an understatement. I didn't know right then, but not only was that text going to impact my day, but it also was going to impact that week, that month, and what would turn out to be the next few years as well. Tuesday, February 4th started what was the toughest four years of my life.

LT had mentioned in his text that he'd sent an email. I didn't open it until I got to the office later that morning. The email was short and simple. Bank names, account holder's names, and account numbers. It instructed me what accounts got what money. Depositing cash into someone's random bank account used to be allowed. It isn't anymore, but it still was back then. LT didn't care if I deposited money with cash or check, neither did the bank.

In all, I was asked to hit eight total banks in the Denver area over the next several days depositing different amounts. All the names and accounts, each of the eight were different banks. A few banks I was instructed to hit on back-to-back days and deposit into different accounts than I did the day before. He had a system down, and he had every dime mapped out. He had a plan to have the full $50,200 paid off by Friday of that same week. That was the $50,000 bet, plus 10% juice (you pay on a losing bet) that's $5,000 minus the $4,800 I had in my virtual account from the playoff run.

I opened another browser on my computer that morning and logged into my own bank accounts that showed $600 in savings, and roughly $1,400 in checking. I had a credit card with a cash advance limit of $1,000 and my 401(k) had another roughly $15k in it. That account would probably take at least a week or so to get access to those funds. I hadn't answered LT's text or email, and I was internally wrestling a couple different emotions. Bits of rage, anxiety, fear and of course, a few moments that I'll never forget when I absolutely busted out laughing at how fucked, I was.

I sent him a text around noon saying that I was gathering money and would need a few days to comply with his email. It was answered immediately with a hasty message that read, "This isn't the deal. Please make your first deposits today!" I didn't reply, nor did I hit any of the banks on Tuesday's list. I was repeatedly texted, called and emailed. Each message was a little more intense. You could feel the emotion through each message. I had already pissed off LT, and I hadn't even had dinner yet on day one.

By Wednesday morning, I was completely ignoring my phone. Just 24 hours after my first message from LT, I was already in the position of ignoring every call coming in. I came up with another $500 and made a deposit of $2,500 in total to one of the accounts from his list around lunch time. I had cleared out all the available cash to my name. The amount deposited wasn't a total from his list, but I thought he'd see a deposit and call off the dogs. I was wrong. About an hour after the single deposit being made of $2,500, I received a text message from him that read, "What the Fuck is this????"

All the communication from him went from irritated, to pissed off, and finally each message you could sense he was angry. The messages and phone calls didn't stop either. They started Wednesday morning and by Wednesday afternoon, I had to stop working and focus on getting some money. I should have gone to Circle K and bought scratch tickets or stopped by the river next to my office and tried maybe gold panning. Those were as good as any ideas as I could come up with.

I had the slightest feeling back in Vegas that if by some weird chance the Broncos lost, this is how this ordeal was going to go down, but that was then, and that feeling was unrealistic and unknown. Now, three days later, I can without any doubt tell you, it was way worse than what I had imagined back in Vegas. I was in the middle of hell, trying to find a way out.

I once read that there are two types of pain in the world. The pain that hurts and the pain that alters. More on this later, but I was half tempted to call LT and offer my ass for a proper beating rather than go through this hell. After all, bruises and scrapes could heal, this money mess may set me back forever. I sat at my office desk all afternoon filling out online applications for loans. I didn't own a home, already had most credit cards maxed or close to it, and I had a hefty car loan. Add that all up and a slight bit of credit issues, well, I got ZERO money offers back on the four or five loans I tried to acquire. The 401k access was a compete fiasco of rules and reasons I had to lie my way through to get. As I thought, it was a pain to get, and it was going to take 7-10 business days before I received the funds. That ass beating from LT was looking more and more like the better option.

Thursday morning on my drive into the office, I called LT, and he answered the phone pleasantly. I was kinda in shock and was immediately disarmed. We were almost like two friends who just had a disagreement and were trying to work things out. He was cool and asked what was going on and I told him I didn't have funds today, but I have 401k money coming in a week or so. His response was better than I expected. "Do you think you can have me the funds by next Friday?"

I responded with the truth, or at least a partially true tail. "They said it would be 7-10 days. I can send you the email with the 401k sell off information that you can verify." I didn't mention it wasn't for the full amount that I owed. Oops.

"Not needed. I appreciate the call. $47,700 is what I have down correct?" He had it down to the penny. "Let's just talk next Friday."

And that was it. That easy, or at least so I thought. All that was easy was the nine-day less stressful reprieve on the monies owed. What I really had was one week to come up with $47,700. After getting the 401k funds, which were taxed by the way, I had a little over $10k coming in a week and a half. Did I mention how fucked I was?

On Friday, I called my pal Abu and asked to borrow $500. There was a $200 tourney that I could win $5k, maybe $6k up in the hills at the casinos of Black Hawk. I finished 15th that night, they paid 13. The other $300 was for Saturday's tourney. That one is also a little bigger and on various Saturdays, you could win $8k to $10k. I went out 20-something and they paid 17. Sunday morning, that same weekend I took a pistol to a pawn shop open on Sundays and got $400 for it. Sunday afternoons they have another $200 tourney. I fired two entries into that thing before busting out of the money again.

I had used my entire weekend to play poker non-stop, three entire days in hopes of generating a little working bankroll. About 30 hours of poker on loans and pawns and each day resulted in zero gains. All I wanted was something, anything that could help me generate some extra money. Sunday night, maybe 9-ish, I finally laid down in bed feeling as tired and defeated as I ever felt in my entire life. Before dozing off, I thought about the tough weeks and months ahead, and could only laugh. Little did I know how tough it was going to be.

# 13

# Miami

*"Everybody has a plan until he gets punched in the face!"*
—Mike Tyson

AS I'VE MENTIONED EARLIER, the options for depositing into random checking accounts at this point were pretty easy. Walk in with cash, a name, and an account number, and your business was done. That's the way LT and I liked it. Very little paper trail, and the banks always provided a receipt. That was going to change before LT, and I finished business though. Banking, especially deposit laws, changed in the last several years, and depositing cash into random bank accounts isn't allowed anymore. You know, the whole money laundering and say, paying off bookies, is frowned upon by the feds.

Anyway, after the Super Bowl I made my original payments, two of them for an even $10k and about 2 weeks later than I originally told LT on the phone that Thursday following the game. Two payments each, both $5k into two different accounts that were from his original list. He was a little upset that it was two weeks late, but he was happy that his payments were finally coming in. He didn't know it then, but that was the end of the money and our relationship. I had nothing left to offer and the best I could do was go dark. Or so I had thought. It would take a little time for me to pick this little detail up, but LT wasn't messing around.

I was traveling a ton for work, some weeks for only a night or two, but for many weeks I was on the road all week long. This works well when you don't want to be found. One day I was sitting at the airport in Denver and was mindlessly scrolling through Facebook. I ran across a feature on the site that on the front end of playing with it appeared harmless. You could tag a travelling destination, say Las Vegas, and Facebook would broadcast a little airplane with a map showing everyone on your feed where you are traveling from and to where. I'm not sure why I was doing it, but it kinda became my thing for a couple of years. I'd schedule a trip, wake up the day of, head to the airport, get checked in, and while waiting to board I'd open the app up and tag my travel plans. Pretty stupid in retrospect. If someone wanted to break into your house, all they needed was some idiot to tell the world he was leaving town. I did it really to update some friends, and have some fun recording my trips for review in later years. I also wanted to let Mom know where I was heading, she actually enjoyed it. She'd get excited just following my post and seeing where I was heading next. I'm not sure which trip of mine that I first posted the "travel" update, but I surely know the last time I did it. That would be to Miami, Florida.

I was working on a couple projects at the time and was in south Florida often. It's a great place to visit. I was down just about every other week for a couple months and anytime you opened Facebook, you could find my little airplane flying from DIA to Miami. This is probably a good time to mention that I hadn't talked to LT in almost six months. Trust me, he wanted to talk often, I just ignored him and blocked his number.

This trip, I had been down for almost a week. One of the projects I was working on was a theatre in a major mall. Again, no names, but let's just say it's one of the larger malls, and one of the cooler theaters you'll ever visit. In Miami or not, the entire place is unbelievable. Nothing but Miami glam everywhere you went. Every single shop or business within the mall was the same. All of it was class, and the theater was nothing short of Ritz quality.

For anyone that is in construction, or who understands the construction business, you probably don't need an explanation. For all you other readers, I feel obligated to tell you a couple tidbits about construction and my experience in Miami. I'll get to LT in just a second.

The theater project was on the fourth floor of this brand-new mall. Most of the construction was to be wrapped up late fall, a little time before the holiday season. The construction rush was in full swing in July and August to make the holiday turnover schedule happen. I and the other several thousand workers (yes, it was a small hard hat army down there daily) were battling to meet deadlines. Of course, we also were battling a few other things. The parking, elevators, the heat, humidity, and even the toilets.

It was downtown Miami, or close enough that finding parking was a daily grind. The mall's parking garages weren't always open and when they were, they rarely opened to construction traffic. Bringing supplies or carrying toolboxes from your truck or rental van that you parked three blocks away was tough. Really, really tough. If you were lucky enough to get something close, you could get unloaded, make your way through the loading dock, and wait in line for at times 20 to 30 minutes for the only two working elevators for the entire mall to get a lift up four floors. Some days you'd have to unload a tractor trailer's worth of goods and stage them on the dock waiting to load, then unload 1/20th of the product, one elevator up at a time, all the while crews from another 100 groups were doing the exact same thing. Sounds brutal right? Well just hold on.

If you haven't ever had to use the bathroom on a construction site, ohh boy the absolute hell you have missed in life. This is a major construction site that is being built from the ground up. Power, water, and yes, bathrooms just don't magically appear. My company didn't get to the site until about 70% of the building's construction was complete. Still, your power needs were iffy, and there wasn't running water, much less porcelain to park your ass on in the event you needed a #2 break. That morning, I had required a #1 and hit the porta-potties in the back hallway on level four. There were three in total, green porta-potties at the end of this long hallway. I had smelled something odd the second I got to the site, but I thought the smell was just an army of construction workers all sharing the Miami humidity, sweating away in close proximity with only the warm, natural air movement available. That was part of the smell, but not all of it.

I approached the door of the first porta-potty. These were four stories up, and I couldn't imagine they were serviced on any kind of regular cleaning schedule. It was later confirmed that they were only serviced when they were full. Ah, yeah. Anyway, I stood there for a brief second staring at the doors to each potty. The little sign on each handle all read vacant. Possibly that was good news, and I had my choice. Which hell hole was I going to pick though?

It was only a brief second, maybe two, but something told me that door number two was the better selection. Nervously I opened the door like I was expecting some clown to jump out with a red balloon and scream "Boo!" There wasn't a clown, but something else jumped out. An aroma that is hard to put into words. We've all had eyes burning when cutting fresh onions. Well, it was almost that fast. I shut that door without stepping inside and grabbed ahold of door number three just to the right. It had to be better.

Prior to opening the door to the second porta-potty I had

mustered up the mindset to just deal with the smell and go in and pee. I truly stopped for a second and thought about this decision. I turned my head away, breathed in a deep breath and stepped inside. I didn't look down. It didn't want to see what might be in the pool of God knows what beneath the toilet seat creating the smell. Something lurked beneath in the green pool of toxic residue, and I had a job to complete. I could be in and out in a minute, maybe less. A second wave of stench arose and as hard as I tried to fight it, it almost got the best of me. I was gasping for breathable air like a fish flopping on a fishing pier just having been pulled out of the water.

I was peeing as fast as I could. A fireman's hose doesn't push that much pressure. I probably did some kind of permanent damage to the lining of my urethra as I was blasting away. Then, mid-stream it dawned on me, the velocity of urine was mixing the deadly chemical below and bouts of new and additional aromas filled the air in my little toilet gas chamber. I almost cut the tip off my little guy speed-zipping my pants back up and I know I didn't finish peeing before spotting my pants. I didn't care; I had to get the hell out of there. My first and only trip to those porta-potties had come and gone.

That same day, I decided to find another place that I could use. I wasn't going to get caught in the position of needing to use one of those things again, ever! During lunch, I noticed a Burger King just across the street. Perfect. I checked it out, and minus needing to show a security guard my proof of purchase to use the bathroom every, single, time; it was somewhat clean, and the water was flushable. BK worked well, minus having to use the elevators in and out of the site. One pee break could take you 45 minutes to an hour, each time.

During the next two months or so, I got to know the security guards well. They had a guard shack on the dock, and nobody could get in or out without passing the station. Everyone, including guests and business owners that went in, had to

96

present a badge. That included all trades or even new team members to your group. They all had to get checked in and go "through the process." One day I received a call that I wasn't expecting.

"Shawn, this is Gabe at dock #1. You have a visitor." He was one of the security guards who had my phone number.

On any given day, I'd get that kind of call from Gabe or another security guard. Day in and day out, I'd get calls from all kinds of Miami area codes. My company was supplying and installing restaurant equipment and furniture for the massive theater. I had all kinds of trades and skilled laborers that we had hired to complete various parts of the project. Plumbers, electricians, welders, etc. Some days I'd hire a dozen labor-ready guys who all had my number wanting me to come get them a badge at the security desk and let them get to work. To say I used the elevators often and got to know the security guards well is an understatement.

"Gabe, did the guy say who he's with?" I answered Gabe's call with a question.

I wasn't alarmed (yet), but oddly I got the call about 2:30 in the afternoon and I wasn't expecting anyone else for the day. Most crews get to the job site around 6 a.m. and are wrapping things up after 2:00. I went for the elevators and had to wait 15 minutes for a spot for the trip down. Gabe rang my phone again.

"Shawn, this guy is demanding to see you now. Are you in route?"

"What's his company's name?" I replied irritated. "I'm moving as fast as I can!"

Gabe replied to my question. "I asked him, and I think he said DB4. Also, the guy is in loafers and a golf shirt. He's not wearing any safety gear. You know the rules; we are not going to allow him on site!"

DB4, hmm? What, or better yet, who the hell is that? Standing, waiting my turn in line, I noticed that I had missed a few other calls in the past couple of hours or so. One from my boss in Denver, and the other I missed three times from the same number. All placed within the past 45 minutes. Somebody wanted to talk with me, and they never left a message. Odd. The job site is normally hammers, drills, and power tools from early morning until late afternoon. If you wanted to make a call, you had to leave the site. Having a conversation, much less hearing a phone ring doesn't usually happen. I wanted to call the number back, but I chose not to.

I was next in line for the elevator when something odd tickled down my spine. Nervousness crept through me like I couldn't quite explain. I knew DB4 but I couldn't get my head around where from. I've seen or heard this term or name before, but where? I stood there waiting for my turn, now actually sweating for another reason. My heart began to beat just a tad harder. Why, I wasn't sure, but I stepped out of line and called Gabe again.

"Gabe, this is Shawn. Can you describe the guy who's waiting for me?"

"Yeah, he's some asshole that doesn't belong here!" That's all he said before he hung up.

DB4, why do I know that? I walked around the upper part of the mall for a minute. More like 15 minutes. Most crew members were packing up and heading home for the day. The mall, still open to construction, was starting to empty of sound. Eerie noises and the sound of a light Miami breeze in the mall was all I could hear. That, and my heart beating harder and harder with each footstep.

DB4 LIFE! That was his logo. I hadn't seen it for years, but LT launched this cheesy website the same year as Superbowl 48. You didn't have to call an agent, you could jump online, place a bet, and they would send you a confirmation email, or call you to confirm your bet. I did it like twice, but it was slow and to be truthful, I didn't want a paper trail. Rather, I didn't want a reminder of what I was doing.

In the upper left corner of the website was the acronym DB4 Life. His office was in Texas, but the logo had some palm trees and a water oasis. DB4 Life meant Daily Bets for Life! It hit me like a strong wind. Once I recalled where I had seen the acronym, I got dizzy and almost fell over. Some level of nervousness came over me like I hadn't felt before. I was weak in the knees, and it was only a minute, but immediately I had to leave the building. Heart racing and sweating like I'd just swam the Atlantic, I was getting out without using the elevator and I for sure wasn't passing that dock today. Perhaps never again.

On the far side of the mall was construction on other retail shops. I ducked into more half-constructed rooms and found staircases and hallways that often led to nowhere. I kept looking for maybe 30 minutes and found an exit-only staircase to the ground level. Every single person coming at me I took note of. I was looking for a golf shirt and loafers. That was my only description of the man. Other than that, I had no idea who I was looking for. Or rather, who was looking for me.

Finally, an exterior exit-only door to the street below. I was out of the mall and on foot to my hotel. You'd think that might have relieved some nerves, but it only escalated things. Every other guy on the streets of Miami was wearing a golf shirt and loafers. I swear everyone there was after me. I wasn't running, but if speed walking was an Olympic event, I would have won a gold medal that day. I had this sick vision circling in my head that every other Cuban-looking man was some hit man named Tony Montana from the movie *Scar Face*. I was a dead man speed walking.

I was in my hotel for maybe 30 minutes before my phone rang again. It was the same number as the calls that I had missed three times earlier. I didn't know who this was, but I wasn't picking this call up either. The phone stopped ringing and after about a minute, it notified me that I had received a new message. The message was from someone who spoke clearly. It was a man's voice. He used my name almost pleasantly, like a friend would. Except I didn't know this guy. He didn't even leave his name, only a message. It still gives me chills just thinking of it. "Shawn, you need to call LT. We are getting our money!" I never once used that Facebook travel feature ever again!

# 14

# I Got the Message

*"If you think nobody cares if you're alive,*
*try missing a couple car payments."*
—Earl Wilson

BEFORE I BOOKED THAT BET I was warned that pay day was Tuesday. That was 2 days after Superbowl 48. Well after almost two years, I had only paid LT $17,000. Avoiding some bill collectors is easy. Easy because we have laws in the US that protect people like me, the consumers who get into trouble. Bookies though? They don't operate with laws, but I still upped my game and continued to run and hide. I was determined that I could outlast or outplay LT. I wasn't paying him any more money. I would have taken that side bet, not paying any more money, and of course I would have lost that bet as well.

Roughly two years into it, my boss walked down the hall at the company where I was working and asked to see me in his office. Great guy, great stories and always a man I've enjoyed working for. His mood was off, and little did I know I was about to hear something unpleasant and frightening at the same time.

Part of my job is to be out in the field quite often and working with customers outside my office. It's not uncommon to be out of the office for days, maybe even weeks on end. So, me not being present when I had visitors was a good thing. Anyway, I was informed by my boss that I had some visitors that had been in a time or two and they didn't seem to have any restaurant needs (my line of work). Rather, they were kinda rude with the front door staff and often sat in the parking lot for hours on end. My boss wanted to know if I was dealing drugs or something and who these idiots were. And I truly didn't know. Even though it was an honest answer, somewhere in the back of my mind something wasn't right, something was off. I had the sense that it was some legal papers being served; but just maybe, perhaps that jackass from Miami?

At the same time, I wasn't answering a single call from any number not assigned to a contact in my phone. If you were calling, I'd only answer if I knew 100% who it was it was. Not the greatest sales technique if you were a salesman, but I didn't want to talk with LT. I did become a master at following up calls later in the day if a legitimate business call had left a message.

Driving into the office even became an entirely different experience. I'd take the second exit and backtrack towards the office so I could pass the parking lot and quickly check if any random cars were populated with goons inside waiting to greet me. Occasionally I also traded my car with my girlfriend, as she drove a complete POS and I wanted to be a "cool boyfriend." Truth be told, if someone knew what I was driving, they might only stop if they saw it in the parking lot. This went on for about three months before I finally snapped and needed to do something. What was it I did, you ask? Here's some options for you to choose from: A) I called LT and put fears and anxiety aside and worked something out; B) Quit a good job and went to work across town.

If you answered A, I love you and thank you for the positive hope that I did the correct thing, but that would have been too easy. So yeah, I had someone reach out at random one day to me and offer me a job. Accepting it would offer another layer of protection and I could possibly return to my work and professional life to a little more normal than what I was dealing with for months on end prior.

My new job offered some great perks. One was that I'd be on the road for days and weeks on end. I wasn't around town often and I could avoid "bumping" into someone who might be looking for me. I received a pay increase and was making progress on some bills that I was behind on. I hadn't talked with LT in a long time, and things looked like they were changing for the better. Or so I thought.

Right around April, a full two-plus years after welching on that bet, life would forever change for me and how I went forward with certain aspects of my life. I received a call from a family member. A close, close, close family member. This family member was at work in the hospitality industry, and they had a very friendly run-in with someone who I knew. Anyway, I got a call one afternoon, just a "how ya doing" kind of call with just a mix of pleasantries. And before we hung up, there was one last detail shared that still spooks me today. "Oh, by the way, some guy bumped into me and said hello. He said he's been trying to find you because you are old football buddies or something. He asked that I tell you he said hello. His name was Larry, or LT. He said you would know who he was and would love to chat sometime."

Thinking about that phone call still makes me sick in my stomach to this day. I can laugh more about it now, but at that time, it was no laughing matter. I had inadvertently brought that man and this nasty part of my life into a loved one's life. Immediately I confirmed the name, but hearing LT's name being repeated didn't help anything. This was the end of the line with all the games and running that I had been doing for far too long.

It was probably an hour before I broke down and texted.

He had sent a clear message, and I couldn't screw around any longer. My plan to outlast and just have this go away evaporated immediately. I had his number; actually, I had several numbers for him from the many lines that he had been calling over the past two years. I texted him that evening with a simple, "Can I call and talk with you at 9 a.m. sharp tomorrow?" His text response back was immediate and almost chilling. "Looking forward to it. 9 a.m. sharp!"

I think I woke up the next day at six. I was up tossing and turning for the better part of the night, but I finally arose and got to work on my speech early. I've been to divorce court, hospitals for bad news, cemeteries for worse news, I had an IRS audit that was horrible, but I've never in my life been as nervous as making that call. I ran through everything in my head trying to come up with a good excuse or how I was going to try and get out of this jam. Each time I came back to the same reality. I was in trouble.

Surprisingly, LT answered the phone in a soft voice, his tone almost sounded kind. Not the way I had envisioned this going down at all. He didn't even say hello and just jump started the conversation with a question. "Who are you betting with these days?"

I responded with the truth. "Nobody. Not a single bet since the Super Bowl."

He continued. "Who else do you owe money to?"

Again, I answered honestly and told him who I owed and what amount. There were no bookies, no other guys, just some credit cards, loans, and a car payment. Still being kind, he asked me what my plan was to square this up. Again, I answered truthfully and said, "I have no money, LT!"

Then the conversation went weird. After a few rounds of what the f@&k is my problem, how could I have done this, blah blah blah, I was asked to fork over my checking account access information. He wanted to verify my story. I figured what the hell. I could call the bank in 30 minutes and get new account numbers, change passwords, get new debit cards if necessary. We were still on the phone while he was digging on his computer verifying my story. What I was paid bi-weekly, how much was going out and to what. Odd, without a single question about our problem, he only mentioned he would call back in an hour, and I needed to answer the phone. It was what you might expect, a long-ass hour.

In less than an hour, LT did return with a phone call. Again, oddly he was pleasant, more or less just doing business. No threats, nothing harsh, only a couple questions. The one question I was asked that I still remember today and might for quite some time was this. "How bad do you want this to go away?"

"Badly," was my answer, and I was hoping he had a plan that worked as I was out of options.

"This is what we are going to do. Your total loss was $55k. I've got the $17,000 already paid. Each month I'm going to send you where you are dropping $2,000 into an account. Every month, for the next 24 months. Any questions?"

I had nothing to add. I had nothing to negotiate. I was stuck, and all I could say was yes. In total, that bet cost me $65,000. I knew the extra amount was what a bank would call interest. This was bookie kind of interest, and that is the worst kind. He made a small joke and left me with some parting words. Remember when he said, "We are getting our money!" The reality is I was out of options; I just wanted this all to go away.

A Robin Williams story I read one time talked about him being in rehab with a bunch of doctors and lawyers. You know the type, the smart kind of people. Well, those types also make mistakes in life, and what Robin noticed was that intelligent people have a little larger-than-normal egos, and the bigger the ego the harder it is for you, or anyone for that matter, to let go. Let go of whatever issue that has ahold of you, that is.

I'd kind of fancied myself as being smarter and being more stubborn than someone like LT, and could "win" against him. What I would discover was he only revealed the simple truth. My ego was in the middle of getting its ass kicked and I only noticed it too late. As tough as this circumstance was, and as tough a deal as this was going to be, my new truth was this. For the first time in over two years, after making the deal, I went to bed that night and slept like a baby.

# 15

# Smothered

*"I try to make sense of things, which is why, I guess, I believe in Destiny. There must be a reason that I am as I am."*
—Robin Williams

LONG, LONG BEFORE THAT FATEFUL DAY back on Super Bowl Sunday in Vegas, I'd done some off the wall things in respect to gambling. You've read the stories from some earlier days, but I'd graduated to a little more sophisticated way of torturing myself and my bank account as I got older. I wanted to include a few other adventures as I believe we are a product of what we do.

The ancient Greek philosopher Aristotle had a famous one liner that read, "we are what we repeatedly do. Excellence then, is not an act, but a habit." Well, if that's the case, then the opposite must be the same and unfortunately, true as well. If it's a habit, not a single act, something like gambling will often lead you to the opposite of excellence.

This isn't the poor-me part of the story, nor do I want to ever have anyone I know, including anyone reading this, think I'm looking for sympathy. That's not my point for writing this or how I want you to read this chapter. However, I wanted to share with you what, for me, that struggle had looked like. For anyone out there that might also have a gambling issue or say perhaps another issue, I see you. I had owned my own issue, and this is the chapter I'll at least try and explain what fueled my gambling problem. I've already shared with you where this little gambling journey began way back in my teens, and where it's been and where it might be going.

Sometime around the poker explosion in the late 90s, my then-wife and I wanted to have a little party at our house. It was the second home we had purchased together, and we wanted to get some family and friends over for a little night of fun. We chose a poker tournament theme for two reasons. The first reason was because poker was everywhere. It was hot, the thing to do either online or in person. It didn't matter; it was in the news, on just about every TV network had some version of a poker game on. In short, it was popular with everyone. The second reason was that in our first house a few years prior, we had a Saturday night party with the same kind of group of invited friends and family, and it was a complete flop. We had all kinds of carnival games, prizes, junk food, cocktails, fun for everyone and we were in bed by 10 p.m. that night. That party sucked by most standards. The poker party, however, a few years later? We had a packed house, played until 2 a.m. and even turned away some friends due to the overcrowding. It was a smashing success.

Just about the same time frame, poker online had exploded, and I was hooked to say the least. Both my wife and I had our own online accounts, and we posted real money on occasion on the poker sites. Her occasion was maybe once or twice a month. Say $25 here and there. My deposits were more like every week, sometimes multiple days in that week, and often more than $25 we had budgeted. It was certainly more than we could afford. As I mentioned before, I wasn't new to gambling, and even though for many years I was out of the poker world, it was now coming to find me in the comfort of my living room. I would have never admitted or even known back then, but I was smack dab in the middle of a gambling problem.

A buddy called me on Sunday morning of Super Bowl 34 that next January and neither of us had anything planned for the game. The St. Louis Rams were playing the Tennessee Titans. Neither team had been to the Super Bowl before, nor was either team a likely favorite early in the year to make the game, much less making the game against each other. It offered a weird aspect for not only viewing, but in this case gambling. There was no history with the teams, and one team even had a QB that used to work at a grocery store just a year or two prior, to now playing in the Super Bowl as the starting QB. That's another great story.

I invited my friend over to the house to watch the game with my wife and the kids later that day. He accepted, but that wasn't the only reason for his call. He also was dabbling a little bit in some online gambling, which was new, and he wanted to know my thoughts on his bets. This would end up being the actual first time I ever spoke of or participated in an online sports bet. Sports betting wasn't huge, at least not yet. All these companies doing this type of business were located offshore, which should have been warning sign number one. He had found a site that was taking bets on the Super Bowl, and he called to see what I thought about the game. It was about 10 minutes into our conversation that I had worked up the emotional attachment and wanted to place a bet myself. I'll spare you the details, but getting money on the site was a nightmare. That was the second warning sign that I ignored. I was dealing with foreigners working the site and the 1-800 line offering help wasn't much help at all. I did more attempts at loading a deposit amount (I might also add, while trying to hide this from my wife) and ended up betting against the grocery store QB who ended up winning the damn game. That should have been my third and final clue that perhaps this sports betting thing wasn't for me. Late in the game that day, my wife had questioned why I was so oddly interested in the game. I was sweating like I'd just run a marathon. Anyway, little did she know that our hard-earned money was at work, and working badly as it turned out. My pal had a good time laughing on the couch knowing what was going on. We were looking at each other snickering, like two kids hiding a secret from the teacher. Other than having him over for the game and some laughs at my expense, the entire day was nothing more than a bust.

Roughly a year later, the kids already in sports, here comes poker again. Charity poker tournaments for the school, or club, or sports, all in the name of fundraising. It exploded in popularity, and I received an invite every time. Now, this was a far cry from the days of sending your kids out to sell coupon books door to door or bags of popcorn, thus the popularity. It was actually very effective as the buy-in, normally around $50 was split in half between the prize pool and charity cause. Everyone from your grandmother to the weird janitor guy showed up and the fundraising was normally a big success. I did enjoy it, wrote it off normally as something good for the kids, but it wasn't helping my problem.

Throughout the years, I've also played a few rounds of golf here and there. If you have as well, you know exactly what I'm also about to tell you. Maybe once, but not twice had I ever played golf where betting of some kind wasn't as popular on the course as playing a round itself. It could be on just the round, or an individual shot. Often it was both, and it's as common as swinging clubs. You can bet your ass that scoring on the course is highly contested even amongst the best friends or top clients. Why, might you ask? Well, there's money involved. Want proof? Remember the Honorable Judge Smails in the movie *Caddy Shack*? Well, it's the first time I ever heard of the foot wedge, and I've seen many a man use the same club to "improve his lie."

Moving along the calendar, a little older, but not much smarter, I started working with another company in my trade. On my first trip out of town to see a manufacturer we worked with, they had a night of fun for their invited guests. The theme for the night, you might wonder. You guessed it, casino night. Everything you could want to play, just like a real casino only in a hotel lobby or something similar. It wasn't the last one, either. Over the course of the next several years, there were all kinds of trips, all over the country where the theme was a casino night or poker night, something that involved gambling. Now most of these didn't involve money, but the atmosphere was still there. Like inviting an alcoholic to a bar, it wasn't good for me; and it was awkward if I ever wanted to say no.

One summer around the same time, I was invited by a friend here in Denver to a Saturday full of fun for another charity group. We had agreed to meet at this park where we were going to learn about horses and doing what we could to help save sick and abandoned horses. It's a pretty big deal across the country, and sad. I had no idea. Anyway, that day sounded cool, and after all, horses are great animals so I was in. That Saturday just so happened to be the same day as the Kentucky Derby, the most famous annual horse race in the world. I hadn't put together the race and the fundraiser on the same day prior, but gambling was right around the corner, again! We spent the entire week planning our outfits down to the color of my socks. It looked like a fun outdoor event on a wonderful Colorado spring day. The morning of, I received a call from my friend confirming our meet-up time and of course, "Don't forget the $500 required to place bets." Um, what? That caught me completely off guard. I had no idea prior, but it was a charity deal for this horse rescue where you place bets, just like if you were at the horse race yourself. Half your winnings (if you won) go to the horse rescue and the other half of your winnings go home with you. Basically, half of anything you bet was going to the horse rescue. I hadn't placed a bet on a horse race ever. Not that it matters, but an odd thing about me is that I've never even sat on a horse in my life. Never once, not even at the petting zoo when I was a kid. The closest thing perhaps I knew about horse racing was they go around a track just like a few dog tracks over the years that I've been to. Yes, the betting-type dog tracks. Anyway, that Saturday people were throwing around hundred-dollar bills faster than on a craps table in Vegas. It was a fun day, we had a lot of laughs, but I never hit a single bet. My $500 all went to the Horse Rescue. Through gambling, I was down $500...Again!

That next spring, I hadn't subjected myself to any public humiliation in quite some time, and it was long overdue. Roughly about February, my pal and I were playing cards in his basement, exchanging 100-dollar bills here and there, but not really doing much. It was just us two, the game was boring and before ending the night, we thought back on the good ole days back in college, specifically stunt poker. Next thing you know, we've come up with a bet. The man that loses the next heads-up tournament must run the Boulder Boulder (local marathon here in Colorado) in costume. Needless to say, I had a rubber Superman costume from college, and it still fit.

In 2011, April of that year to be exact, the feds hammered down on the online poker sites. They shut down all the big sites with no warning. It was a Friday; I remember the day well. I had been paid my commission check from work and it was a light month. I needed the funds off the site to pay some bills and wouldn't you know it, the site I played on was shut down. They have never, to this day, EVER paid a cent of that money. At first this really bothered me as I was occasionally winning money, trips, and other "stuff," but years later, I looked back and knew this was truly a gift from God. I never, even today as sites are coming back with real money technology, the online poker experience is dead with me.

For many years, I was traveling a ton for various work projects. If you have ever traveled for work, it can be a little boring not having anyone in town to say, grab dinner with or maybe see something special about that part of the country. Didn't matter where I went, there always seemed to be a casino somewhere close to my hotel.

As a side note, one of my all-time favorite movies is *Dances with Wolves* starring Kevin Costner. One day on the road for work, that movie was playing on one of the flights I was on. Later that day, I explored some online information on the amount of registered Indian lands across the country. I was shocked to say the least. The Federal Government will tell you it's over 500 actual different Indian tribes. Various other parties would tell you it's almost 2,000 in number. If you really dig deep into a few rabbit holes, the amount of land that has been registered as Indian land has exploded in the last several decades. Why just recently, you ask? One common theory perhaps is you guessed it. Gambling. The number of Indian casinos that have also popped up on these "registered lands" a few years later is a little odd.

All of this was circling in my life right about the time leading up to me making that $50,000 bet. This isn't an excuse, but I couldn't escape gambling. It was all around me. If I wasn't looking for it, it would find me. Work trips, school functions, the internet, dating, all of it was becoming too much to handle, almost suffocating. Looking back, I can say the worst part of having a problem is not knowing you have the problem.

I did look in the mirror one day and knew I wanted help, but I had absolutely zero idea where to find it. I was trying to fill my free time at home or on the road with various other things to do, writing being a major one. My first book happened for many reasons; one was to give me something to do rather than gamble. I was watching a video the summer following that big bet and ran across a video interview that I liked. The interview was with Robins Williams, the late, great actor who once commented in an interview that he chose to go to rehab in wine county. Robin was an acknowledged alcoholic who was open with his issue and how he managed it. Anyway, when the reporter asked why he chose wine country for his treatment center? He replied, he "needed options." I'm sure it was said as a joke but having recognized my own issues I can guarantee part of that statement was 100% truth. How odd I place that bet, find that video, and his unfortunate death were within 6 months of one another.

The point I'm trying to make is how I got to where I was, namely by making some decisions in life, especially with money, and gambling wasn't always intentional. As hard as I tried to avoid some things, some things wanted to find me, I guess. I've had many conversations with people who I know and trust, many of which have helped me see the possible light at the end of the tunnel. Everything you go through in life, whether it be some kind of substance abuse, maybe some food/health issues, physical abuse of some kind, or in my case, GAMBLING; whatever it is, it's not void of purpose.

I love the fact that many people in the Bible that God used all had issues. Many great people in the Bible all fell short and, in some cases, did some horrible things. Most of those people went on to have a purpose far grander than how it looked early on in their lives. For me, I'm not there yet, but I'm on my way. Maybe you'll find some wisdom in my struggles, and what exactly I did to get through some tough days.

# 16

# FedEx

*"Money will buy you a fine dog,*
*but only love can make it wag its tail."*
—Richard Friedman

"WHAT WERE YOU THINKING?" I wasn't there that day, but somewhere in the middle of a conference room, tucked away in corporate America, everyone on the board all asked Fred the same question. It wasn't probably the first time he had heard the question, and probably wasn't the last time either.

Who else has heard that question before? I'm guessing we all have. A fair question applied to so many parts of our lives. Not just in gambling, either. Me? I've heard it before, and I'm sure I'll hear it again. I've come to grips with it actually and have learned not to take that kind of question as an insult, or a question of my character. Oddly, those who ask it seem to have more character flaws than I do.

Anyway, the first time I was asked this question was probably by my mother or perhaps by a teacher many years ago as a kid. I'm sure, like most of us, we can't really recall the occasion. If I thought about it long enough, I probably was questioned the same way in one capacity or another just last month. "What were you thinking?"

Several years ago, I read a story about that exact question being asked by a group of people about a silly decision of one of their own. The question was asked by the executive leadership team and the CFO of FedEx. Who were they asking? You guessed it, FedEx's owner and CEO, Fredrick Smith.

In the early 70s, FedEx was launched and from day one was doing some odd things in the world of shipping. Good things, but odd in the sense that nobody else was doing them. Fred started FedEx with an idea of not moving people, but rather product around the world. Fred had served in Vietnam and noticed something missing in the supply chain industry globally.

Like most companies long before FedEx and plenty of others since, they had their share of struggles. FedEx was struggling from day one to say the least. Actually, describing FedEx as a struggling company in the early years is probably a gross understatement. At one point, before they ever achieved the milestone of earning a million dollars a month, they were losing a million dollars a month. Rumors were circulating not just in the airline industry but around Wall Street that painted a grim picture of the struggling company. Some of those rumors were that FedEx pilots used personal credit cards to pay for fuel at various airports to fuel for the next leg of the flight. Others reported that employees across the company were issued paychecks that they couldn't cash. The company was bleeding money. The positive was it seemed from these rumors, was that there were employees everywhere doing anything and everything to help the company out. Everyone believed in the company and the man running it.

FedEx was a new business model, and this was a company with a different idea, but it was operating in the red. Before he opened the doors, Fred had written a paper in college about his FedEx vision and received a C+ from his instructor. I would love to read that paper today. I often wonder what great vision was in that paper that at the time was scoffed at. I also jokingly wonder if his professor wrote a question along with the C+ grade they had given Fred, "What were you thinking?"

The stories continued for a few years about the radical and creative steps necessary to keep the shipping company in business. FedEx was in and out of trouble with creditors for years in the early days. Fred and his executives working every angle possible were in and out of meetings, traveling to wherever and with whomever could possibly lend a hand. As the days and debts mounted, desperation was also mounting.

Following another funding trip to Chicago, Fred made a call to the company's CFO inquiring to the current state of the union within the company. The news was worse than what was expected. From the airport in Chicago, he cancelled a trip home and went west with a different idea. Las Vegas, Nevada was his impromptu destination, following yet another failed attempt in Chicago to secure funds to keep fuel in his planes.

His Vegas meeting wasn't anything like his prior business meetings over the last year. He wasn't dealing with partners, bankers, or investors. He wasn't selling shares, and certainly wasn't offering any of this for any of that. His planned meeting didn't require spreadsheets, business forecasts, debt sheets, or signatures on promissory notes. There wasn't a proposal of any sort, and a presentation was not required. The meetings in Vegas only required cash.

It was the end of the week, and his CFO had just told Fred that FedEx had plus or minus $5,000 available in the corporate checking account. They couldn't make payroll; creditors were calling and every lease signed on any property was due. Worse, planes don't work without fuel so buying time wasn't an option.

FedEx was literally down to nothing. In the next couple days, FedEx would be bankrupt and out of business. They might not even make Monday just three days away. Sitting in Chicago, Fred had an idea and launched an emergency plan. Fred's meeting was at a high limit blackjack table in Las Vegas, Nevada.

Where exactly he played and what happened at the table(s) that weekend has always been under wraps. Perhaps a friend, someone within the family, or maybe that CFO, but that's it. The who, how, where and why between Friday night and Monday morning have always remained quiet.

On the following Monday morning, however, the FedEx checking account had $32,000. An uptick of $27,000 over the weekend and not a single business check was deposited. The money came from somewhere else. It came from Fred and his work in Las Vegas. That deposit kept the ball rolling just long enough to gain some momentum. By the end of the year, FedEx had cleaned up some bad debt and was making money. By the end of the decade, FedEx had crossed the 50-million-dollar mark. Today, FedEx is valued at over 50 billion dollars.

50+ billion dollars. The best word that comes to mind is WOW. I think of this story often. When I find myself down in the dumps or down on my own luck. This story brings a smile to my face and warmth to my heart. One of the good guys took a shot and won. One man willing to do just about anything to save his idea, his business, maybe the last opportunity to save his dream.

I've heard of a few other nutty stories, but this is the biggest one. The amount of money gambled wasn't the story. After all, it was only around $5,000. What made this story is how that $5,000 saved a business and how big that business became. FedEx today has +/- 700 airplanes all over the world. All those planes are named after the children of employees working at FedEx. How cool is that? One big, happy family. How many lifesaving operations, or desperately needed supplies, or a document that would launch another billion-dollar company might not have happened if Fred didn't take a chance? That's the one question that really plagues every businessperson, and most gamblers. It has and still bothers me today. "If I don't take a chance……..."

I find it funny that a new high school graduate can walk into any bank in America and ask for a loan. Most new or first-time business loans are for less than $15k in the USA according to the Small Business Association. Perhaps that graduate needs a few bucks to start up a tech business. Maybe the money is needed for an environmental solution? Maybe it's only a little funding for a restaurant and their idea is how to feed people better and cheaper. Of course, the bank will do all the required paperwork, they might even photocopy IDs, you know all the normal banking "stuff." That 17- or 18-year-old won't get the loan, though. Work history is what they'll probably be told. Or my favorite reason for denial, they won't have the credit, creditworthiness they call it.

Take that same kid, same idea, just derail it and tell them to spend a few years in college first. That'll help, they'll say. They can build up some more work experience; perhaps get a little more business savvy while waiting tables. I did it, nothing wrong with it. One little detail or side part of this plan though? The average US college graduate leaves with their diploma and just short of $30k in debt! What a backwards-ass system.

Another backwards system and my personal favorite (yes, I've had this happen to me) is the tale of $10,000. After a divorce in 2005, I started a new job and re-started investing in one of those online investment corporations. It wasn't a company 401(k) plan at my job, but something I was doing on my own. Hold on to this part of the story.

Roughly a year or so later, I had a business idea and needed some money. Not much, I applied for a $10,000 loan. I had cleaned up my credit, had a solid work history, references out the wazoo, bought a condo, and even managed to save a few dollars. For my business plan I just need a few extra dollars to get my idea off and running. The idea wasn't important, but the tale of two $10,000 investments is. Stay with me here.

The fine print at the bottom of the investment prospectus, any investment prospectus always reads the same. The short words read, "Profit or proceeds are NOT guaranteed." Translated, you may take a loss on your $10,000. They'll do their best, but if "things don't work out," well your $10,000 could be lost to the volatile climate or nature of investing. You will have zero recourse to retrieve any such monies invested.

The fine print on the bottom of the loan I took out, read just a little differently. "You will be personally responsible for this money, all associated costs, and the interest agreed to upon receiving the loan." I'll paraphrase, but further, if something volatile happens in your world, or something unknown causes a situation for you to not be able to pay the loan back, we, the lender, will invoke all the laws known to man to come after you, and collect every dime you borrowed.

In 2007 I started that little business, and like Fred and FedEx, I was struggling. I was co-parenting with my former wife while working three jobs. My primary 40-hour a week job was in the design and consulting industry. I had a part-time job as an adjunct professor at a community college two nights a week, and on Saturdays about two or three times a month, I helped manage a poker room at a casino in Black Hawk. I'm not sure how, but for 2 hours a week, I even volunteered at the kitchen at the hospital right down the road from my condo. I was balanced in life, but busy was an understatement.

My little start-up side business was struggling, but I was making headway. The loan was 100% helpful. Rather, it was absolutely critical. Without it I was dead in the water. I was at a construction site in southern California when I heard rumors that the Lehman Brothers had or was in the process of folding. They are (or were) some investment house or property investment group funding the hotel project where I was doing work.

Well, that was the summer of 2008. That year the housing market went bust and the economy took a major downturn. A major downturn probably isn't the right term, but it sounds more professional than "shit the bed." And that is exactly what happened. One of the largest recessions and housing bubbles completely imploded and very few, if any, didn't feel the ripple.

My business folded. Then, on December 7th of that year I was laid off from the consulting job. Two weeks later, right before Christmas I was notified that my teaching job would be temporarily suspended due to low student enrollment. Two weeks later in January, the casino was closing the poker room due to the recession. What in the hell just happened? Did I really lose three jobs in 30 days?

2009 was the start of an entirely different set of problems. I had a mortgage, a car loan, a couple credit cards, child support, that $10,000 loan, another bill called food, and no job. What I did have saved up was gone in two months. This isn't that kind of story though, and I'm not bringing this up for sympathy, but the final point to this entire part of the story is this.

When Super Bowl 48 rolled around, I made a bet that I shouldn't have, but it was an opportunity to clean some things up. Catch up on some bills maybe, or perhaps even start that business again. The bottom line is this. When I have been asked, "What was I thinking?" My answer is always the same and probably a lot like Fred's was back in the early 70s. "What other choice did I have?"

# 17

# Sucker Punched

*"Some people are born on third base*
*and go through life thinking they hit a triple."*
—Barry Switzer

I'D BEEN IN A FIGHT A COUPLE OF TIMES as a kid growing up. I think most guys like me probably have. Looking back, very little happened in any of the mix ups. The first time I can recall was when I was maybe 10 or 11 years old. Some kid punched me in the gut, I lost my breath and was rolling around on the ground gasping for air like I was going to die. We all know that feeling, and the fight was over before it even began. A few years later, maybe when I was 14 or so, I was much braver and I punched another kid in the face (he had it coming). And after one shot, he screamed like I had just cut his arm off and ran away as fast as he could. For a brief time afterwards, I thought I was the heavy weight champion of the world.

My last fight was in college in some drunken brawl when a couple idiots got out of line at a party. I thought I'd be one of the heroes and run to the girl's aid who was throwing the party. This one guy, he and I just squared off and started rolling around on the ground both half-drunk not really doing much. I think he tore my shirt, and I might have scratched him. Yeah, we were real tough guys. Many hours later, he and I ended up doing shots together in the same house and we laughed at each other for how stupid we must have looked.

Those days were long ago, and I can thankfully say I have never truly hurt someone, or myself. I could probably just about kill someone if they harmed a loved one, so I've also been lucky there. Hopefully I'll never be in that situation. For the most part, I would consider myself a man whose first instinct is to help, encourage, direct, or correct someone who might be doing something that could either hurt themselves, or God forbid, someone else. I did have something happen a few years ago that for the life of me hurt worse than any punch I've ever had to endure.

Somewhere in the middle of my four years of hell, I reached out to three people. Four, if you include coming clean with the gambling with the woman I was dating at the time. Anyway, the other three individuals I reached out about speaking with them about a problem. My problem with gambling that is. I knew I needed help and thought, who in my life could I trust? I just needed some people to talk with. I didn't need, want, or ask for money from any of them. In one week, I made plans to see each of the three people on my list. I had a co-worker who was probably the most level-headed guy I've ever known. I spoke with him first; maybe on a Tuesday, and we went into depth of what I was doing and why I thought I was doing it. It was a great conversation, he gave me a couple ideas, never said anything that wasn't positive, and he and I are still tight to this day.

The second person I spoke with was my brother. He was quite a different child, but he's grown into one of the better men out there today. He's a faith-centered man and he has his priorities in life in line. He works as a teacher in some rather sketchy neighborhoods. He has more gang members in some classrooms than your average demographic and has been voted by his students as teacher of the year more than once. He's wicked smart in the classroom and even more so out on the streets. If you put a label on him, it would be one smart and tough man. He and I spoke for roughly six hours one night about my issue and it was one of the better conversations I've ever had in life.

The third and final person I selected to chat with was with another lifelong friend. He's a guy who I've known for more than 30 years. Let's call him Leigh. Leigh was actually in my wedding, and I can honestly say I've laughed with this guy in more places, about more things than any other person I know. He's a very successful business owner. He's done well in life. We spoke on Sunday night; it was the last conversation of the week. I'll continue in a minute about this conversation, but first a comment or two.

The morning following my week of confessions I didn't wake up magically cured, but I'll tell you this, I felt a sense of hope that I hadn't felt in a long time. It actually felt really good having come clean with some people. There is a Bible verse in John 8:32 that says, "The truth will set you free." What a great verse and how true that is. I can honestly say that I've never had any other issues with anything else as an adult. I've never been violent or abusive. I know that's funny to read seeing I started this chapter about fighting. Anyway, I've never smoked, never had an issue with drugs or alcohol, and I find strip clubs and porn rather boring. I say these things because I believe it's important to anyone reading this. We all have our issues. Some more than others, but for me some of those conversations reminded me that I'm not a bad guy. At times though, I felt like the worst guy in the world. I've made some mistakes, but I'm doing a great deal more for myself, my family, and friends than I give myself credit for. For anyone out there, perhaps the truth about your issue is all you need to set yourself up on the right path. Not one of those conversations solved the problems I was dealing with at the time but wow, did I feel better having chatted with each of those people.

Most of you reading this book can probably all attest that we have all heard of a young lady named Karma. If you gamble, you probably know her all too well. And if you have heard her name, it's probable that you, like me, have had firsthand experience of a certain little rumor about her. I have firsthand experience a few too many times, unfortunately. Yes, if you know of her, we can all agree that she's a real BI*CH!

What I'd also bet is many of you didn't know she has a twin sister. That's right, she does. Just like her sister, she's equally perfect and beautiful on the outside, but she's also brutally ruthless and unforgiving on the inside. Oddly, the two of them together have done the world and its inhabitants better than any of us would like to admit. And just like her sister, she pays almost all of us a visit at some point in life. For some of us, more than once. Her name? Humility.

There is a saying in both professional sports and in the entertainment industry that is if you haven't been humbled, your turn is coming soon. We could probably all agree that some of our biggest heroes in sports have had moments that weren't very flattering or something anyone would envy. We've watched and at times have cried or felt poorly watching our heroes stumble. Translated? You, me, and everyone out there isn't alone, and we've all had to replace our egos at the great table in life for a better seat. Where do you think the term humble pie came from? It's often fed to you right in front of the world to see. Now back to that third and final conversation.

Leigh, my pal of 30+ years, blessed me with exactly what I had asked. I needed him to give me a friendly ear and hear me out. I just needed a pal who I trusted to talk with. He knew I gambled; it wasn't a surprise to him. Heck I've been to many a casino with the man. That first fantasy football team I told you about earlier. He was one of the founding members. He didn't know until that night what kind of trouble I was in, and even though I was being honest, I didn't let him know the amount of trouble I was truly in when I left his house. I just needed some perspective from a good guy.

It would be some time later after that conversation that both Karma and Humility would be visiting me soon. Karma as we know often pays a visit after we've done something wrong. Humility pays a visit to keep our attitudes, or rather our egos, in check. I never saw it coming, but that same man, a pal of 30+ years of friendship sent them both to me with one text message.

You could call it a sucker punch. I never saw it coming and when it came, as I said earlier, I had never been hit that hard. I've been married once, been in another handful of relationships that ended poorly, played college football and had a few boo boos, and raced motocross and ended up with a heck of a lot more than a few boo boos. I was attacked by dogs when I was eight years old, been stabbed in the stomach (freak accident) and once dropped a 225-pound barbell on my face with stiches to prove it. I've dealt with pain in my head, heart, and body at times equally. Nothing hurt like a text message I was about to read.

I played in a fantasy football league during the middle of those four years of being on the run. I should have never played for two reasons. First, it was pricey, and the guys playing it took it very seriously. The second, I was so busy at the time living a secret life, I didn't prepare or stay on target for anything with consistency. Especially playing in a high-priced fantasy football league. I had thought there was a chance I could win, and that win would net over $10k in profit. I could have really used that money. Plus, it was with some buddies, so why not, I thought. As you can guess when the season was over, I was nowhere near winning and when it came to payday, I was a little short. How much do you ask? Like the whole way.

I didn't have 20 bucks extra at the time. I owed over $2,300 to the league and I was right in the middle of legal problems, debt collectors, IRS issues, a bookie, and job troubles. The weather man would have called it the perfect storm.

Now Leigh, he didn't play in the league. Why? Well probably because he's smarter than me. I say that seriously. He is a busy man in life, and he told me once he couldn't do both. Play and work at the same time that is. He'd rather work hard and concentrate on his business and call his pals occasionally and just say hello. Plus he'd said, why risk losing the +/- $2,000 not putting your "all" into something. He was so right, and often made so many good decisions. See why I wanted to chat with him?

Again, Leigh didn't play that year. But he did keep in contact with another buddy of ours that did. After the season, as I drug on the payment, or rather lack thereof, some of the guys in the league started to lose their cool. I don't blame anyone; I probably would have also been a little hot with some A-hole who shorted or who was not paying the monies owed. I'm not looking for sympathy, never did, nor did I deny owing it, but I was just in a bad spot. All I was really hoping for was some time and perhaps a little grace to get some matters in order.

Out of nowhere, one day I got this text from Leigh. It was about 2:30 in the afternoon. I was driving at the time and noticed a new text message came in from Leigh. We hadn't talked in a couple weeks. It was a little odd, because we normally spoke several times per week. I had left a message or two on a voice mail and perhaps a text during the weeks prior and I didn't think much about him not returning any communication back. I knew we were both busy.

At the next red light, I was stopped and opened the message. It was a good paragraph, and I had to read it twice. I was in complete shock. A few minutes later, I pulled into an empty parking lot and probably read it about five more times, and then a few more times over the course of the next hour or so. It wasn't well written, tons of grammatical mistakes, odd punctuation, and run on sentences. Kinda typical of text messaging with auto correcting I know, but you'd think if you were going to send one of the most judgmental, hateful, and in general, rude messages to a friend of all people, you'd have your words and your message a little better written. What is even odder, this guy was one hell of a sportswriter when he worked for the Rocky Mountain News here in Colorado. I read every single article this guy ever wrote, called his editor at the paper and praised his writing. I shared his work with friends and family alike. He was that good, heck I'm sure he's still that good today. What I received in that text was written garbage!

Leigh had been talking with that other friend of ours in that league. He knew I hadn't paid off the money due. He let me know that he thought me working on myself, improving on things in my personal space while celebrating other people's well-being on social media was what he thought to be in poor taste. He thought I was being hypocritical. What??? He mentioned a few other things, too, that were so poorly communicated that I just had to let it go. I'm sure glad I didn't go to his house that night confessing to a drug or alcohol problem and I'm really glad I wasn't talking about being suicidal at the time. Looking back, he may have handed me a gun. It's been many years, and we have had zero communication since that text message. The unfortunate reality is that we will probably never speak again.

Money is funny. It will change people. I think we all can admit that each of us has had first-hand experience, good or bad, with another person, friend, or family that was damaged because of a loan or debt gone bad. Many people I know, perhaps you as well, often like to quote money as being the root of all evil. Some even say that that quote comes from the Bible.

Well, that's not exactly correct. The Bible does not claim that, nor does it identify money as the underlying cause of all bad things. The actual Biblical verse says, "The <u>love of money</u> is the root of all evil." 1 Timothy 6:10. Many also don't know that in the Bible, there are more talks and discussions of money than there are that of love. Translated? Most of us are going to have issues in our lives because of love, but we are all probably going to have more issues over money.

I still sometimes think of that text and my old friend Leigh. As much as I miss him at times, he had to say goodbye. I hate to admit it, but he introduced me to Humility that day and she has taught me a good lesson. A lesson many of us hear all the time. That message is, cut people off that are bad for your well-being. My ego never thought for a second that anyone I knew would ever have to cut me out of their lives. I never entertained the idea that I was being toxic, or just bad for someone's wellbeing. Leigh needed to say goodbye, not because of what he was doing, but because what I was doing wasn't in line with his life. That's what humility will do. Just like her sister, she serves all of us a purpose.

As much as I wanted to tell my old friend what I thought of him that day, and perhaps even tell him to "Have a nice day" (we know what that means), after some reflection I thought differently. Again, humility at work perhaps. Rather, I chose to think of nothing but the great memories, and good times we shared in the 30+ years I knew the guy. If I ran into him today, or if someone asked what I thought of him, I'd merely say I hope he's well and I have nothing but love for the guy.

Of every experience I've had to deal with during this whole ordeal, this one taught me more than any other. I was blessed to not only know the man for 30+ years, but his biggest gift ever to me was when he said goodbye. I wished it would have been kinder, but sometimes ripping the band aid off is what's necessary. If you're reading this Leigh, I will always thank you for doing what we both probably needed. I wish nothing but the best for you.

# 18

# Save the Rhino

*"Shallow men believe in luck or circumstance;*
*strong men believe in cause and effect."*
—Ralph Waldo Emerson

THERE IS A SAYING IN LIFE, "good things come to those who wait." That is true in poker too, as patience is a top virtue many great players strive for in their game. There's also another saying many poker players know all too well, "good things come to those who re-buy!" Translated, if patience or luck isn't on your side, perhaps your bankroll is and you can re-buy your way through the day. Maybe it was attempt number two, three, or who knows, your tenth re-buy that paved the way to victory. I mention this because it was about this time in life that my bankroll couldn't afford much, and often playing wasn't as they say, "in the cards."

I filled many quiet days with some various other activities. I tried many, but nothing did better for my mind, body and spirit than reading. I have become a very avid reader, but I'd never read anything from ole Waldo. That's Ralph Waldo Emerson, the world-famous writer. I ran across that quote at the beginning of this chapter from him a few years ago and I wanted to include it in this book. I thought it was fitting. I also wanted to include a cool chapter in this project for all the bleeding hearts out there, so this is your chapter. Before I continue, let me also say that if you're not a bleeding heart, you should be.

There's only one man who has won both the WSOP (World Series of Poker) Main Event and the European WSOP Main Event. He's referred to as the Poker Brat as his antics, meltdowns, and otherwise poor behavior at times on the poker felt have made for some pure television gold. Like most, I assume, I love to watch him but at times cringe in doing so. He's been in some of the most epic screaming matches, arguments, and a few fist fights along his career path. If you know poker at all, you know who I'm talking about; you know about the championships, the money, his marketing, you probably know his name. There is no official number or particular stat about the kind of revenue that the Poker Brat and many others like him have generated for the sake of a charity, but they should get much more press than they do. The events are truly amazing, and I thought of sharing some of these incredibly impressive stories.

The Poker Brat is a big bleeding heart. There is a true story out there about when he won his European bracelet back in 2012 that I thought was amazing. At the time, Chinese Poker (a version of another card game), was a big game for some heavy-weight players all around the world. These heavy weights were playing at levels and with stacks of cash that would make even extremely wealthy people nervous. You play and pay or get paid on points. If you are playing at say a dollar a point and lose by 10 points, you would owe 10 bucks to your opponent. Pretty simple to follow don't you think?

Well, I'm not sure who was there or who he was playing that day, but it was reported that the Poker Brat had lost a truck load of money the night before the start of the European WSOP. How big was the truck you might ask? Try over $100,000 in just one evening. Not that that's all that impressive as I know pro players and many wealthy wanna be pros around the world will lose a 100 grand in some cases daily. But anyway, the Brat has an odd catch on this part of the story. It was reported that he was so upset with himself for how bad he was playing and just wasting his money, he was quoted as saying "I was just giving money away" to the many on-lookers. When he lost that night, he settled up with his opponent and went to his hotel room to call his wife. He called her and asked that she immediately write a check to Doctors Without Borders (a great charity by the way) for the same $100k that he had just lost and get it in the mail right away. He was asked later why he did it and was also quoted "If I was going to blow a $100k on a game that I shouldn't be playing, I might as well do some good for the same amount for someone else." A few days later, he won the European WSOP for more than a million dollars.

Pretty cool story, but it's only part of a much larger one. The Brat is estimated at being behind or involved with other groups as well and collectively they have raised over $60 million in all kinds of fund-raising events. That's $60+ million and he's not even number one! He's not alone either, there are many more like him and these are a couple of those stories you might enjoy.

Texas Dolly, the grandfather of poker. If you gamble or play cards, you know exactly who I'm talking about. He was there at the time of the first-ever WSOP and played in most of them along the way. He was literally actively playing until his passing in the summer of 2023. Dolly's list of accomplishments on the poker table is a mile long. Off the poker table and for charity? That list is probably more than a mile long, but one story I find incredibly heartwarming. When you think of Texas, oil wells come to mind. Now Texas Dolly was rumored to have another kind of well, several wells in his background. Early in his playing career he would sponsor the building of water wells in poor, water-starved regions around the world. As a joke, he'd beat you out of your money on the poker table and then use those funds to open another well. He'd name the well after the man he just unloaded his money of. I laugh at the fact there are water wells around the world with the names of defeated poker players who mixed it up with the Texas Dolly and lost. How many kids out there drink water because of Dolly and the world of poker?

Speaking of kids, Kid Poker is another bleeding heart (also a famous professional player) who several moons ago went to work with one of the best organizations in the world. That group is St. Jude, who is leading the way for how the world reacts, treats, and defeats life-threatening diseases in children. If you only ever donated to one group out there, you couldn't go wrong with this one. Anyway, Kid Poker and a few other well-known celebrities started the ONLY official charity poker tournament supporting St. Jude that is still to this day an annual event. The event is called "St. Jude Against All Odds," and has raised millions of dollars for the charity.

Another cool story that I personally experienced a few years back is when I had the privilege of playing (and unfortunately losing) to The Robin Hood of Poker. If you goggled his nickname, you would read some impressive things about this professional poker player. He's a soft spoken, proper gentleman on the outside, but ruthlessly skilled and fearless on a card table. He is a world-class player, the father to six children, four of whom are adopted, and a best-selling author. His philanthropic work for children's organizations around the world is second to none. He once won a tournament that had a first-place prize of better than three quarters of a million dollars. After taxes were paid, the cost of travel and event entry were taken care of, he donated the rest to a children's charity. The sum that day was nearly a half million dollars. Every single time he scores a win, a win of any kind, his favorite charities collect a check. Nobody in or out of the poker circle ever roots against The Robin Hood of Poker.

The stories continue and get even more impressive. I'm sure most reading this have been to Las Vegas. I'm also sure that many of you have been to a Cirque du Soleil show at one of the many properties on the strip. Or perhaps you or someone you know has seen one of the shows in the 40 countries that employ over 4,000 performers each and every year. This guy's nickname isn't well known or important, but his story is. He's a Canadian businessman who started and once owed the Cirque Du Soleil brand. It's a high-class circus that doesn't use animals and their entertainers are world-class. What's also world-class is the businessman's approach to a world health issue. Clean water! He's done all kinds of neat things outside his businesses like travel in space and play poker with the top stars in the world. Several years ago, he convinced the WSOP (World Series of Poker) to make a special tournament that cost a cool ONE MILLION DOLLARS to enter. The first of its kind. The charity was called One Drop Foundation. It provides clean water and hygiene products to places all over the world. The first year they ran the poker event, which sold out by the way, the charity received more than five million dollars for its cause. Not bad for a guy who learned to fire-eat as a kid.

Another fun story, the group Save the Rhino was started on a poker table. In 1970, the rhino poaching epidemic began that hit the black rhino populations severely. The crisis continued to deplete populations right through to the early 1990s, so much so that by 1993, there were only an estimated +/- 2,000 black rhinos left in the world. Founders and rhino enthusiasts, Dave Stirling, Johnny Roberts and Douglas Adams took themselves on a 'Rhino Scramble' across Africa, raising money and meeting many rhino conservationists along the way. Filled with inspiration from their journey, the two returned to the UK, started Save the Rhino International and began raising more money for rhino conservation. The first dollar I ever sent to any animal group was after reading this story.

I ran across this charity after reading about a poker event where one of its participants, a "nobody" in the world of poker finished in second place and gave his portion of the winnings to the Save The Rhino origination. As I read the story, I'm not sure what I was more taken back by. The fact that a group of recreational players pay, compete, and give it all away; or the fact that there are A-Holes out there that buy the horns from a killed rhino. Yup, that's all the value that incredible animal has, and the poaching is still a huge problem throughout the world. Well, that same poker group in London still plays and still donates thousands of dollars yearly to that and other causes alike.

I wanted to include all these stories in the book for a bigger reason. I hope anyone out there reading this understands that getting more in life requires you to be better in life. I know that sounds cliché-ish, but "to whom is given, much is expected." (Luke 12:48). The Bible speaks more of money than love and God himself makes it clear throughout scripture. "Give, and it will be given to you. A good measure, pressed down, shaken together and running over, will be poured into your lap. For with the measure you use, it will be measured to you." (Luke 6:38) "One man gives freely, yet gains even more; another withholds unduly, but comes to poverty." (Proverbs 11:24)

Somewhere in the middle of my mess, that Save the Rhino story found me, and I stepped out in faith and did something about it. After reading that story and doing a little digging about a few people and their groups above, I was determined to be a better man, myself. The stories out there are endless, these are only but a few.

The first group that called to me was in Kentucky, my birth state. They have a charity called the Primate Rescue. The name says it all, and smack dab in the middle of me owing a bookie every single extra cent I made each month, I found a way to write a check and send it off. Something funny happened when I noticed that the bank had processed that check. I wanted to do it again, it felt that good. The next one was to the Elephant Sanctuary in Tennessee. Then the Turtle Hospital in south Florida. St. Jude's Children's Hospital, Doctors without Borders,

The Salvation Army, The Douglas County Animal Shelter, Water for People, and my personal giving list grew.

I started a little deal with myself and proudly have continued it for many years now. I call it the check in and check out plan. I've done checks as little as $5, and as big as $500. Every time I receive money from work or another activity, I send one of my favorite charities a check. I laugh at the fact that I still get on occasion, cancelation notices for various monthly bills before paying them. But I'll be damned if I miss one of those checks going out to a group I follow.

Believe me when I tell you, receiving letters and phone calls from groups out there thanking you for the smallest of gifts is one of the best things you can ever hear or read. Want proof? Try it for a couple weeks; or even just one time, it'll change your life. Pick one of the groups listed above or maybe something near and dear to your heart and donate. Then, in two weeks, do it again! If you're short on cash, give some of your time occasionally to a group or a function. You might even find a charity poker tournament that you can play in that has some big plans for someone or something out there all because of you!

# 19

# Nineteen

*"Being honest may not get you a lot of friends,*
*but it'll always get you the right ones."*
—John Lennon

BRENDAN MCDONOUGH IS A MAN I've never met. Not yet anyway. If you were to search for his name online or anywhere in the media, you'd find plenty of stories, a few short video clips and even a major motion picture with him being a key figure in a major Hollywood production. His story is real. I was having some real fun with the last chapter and ran across this story years back around the same time. This is a horrible story, but a cool one at the same time.

For some time, I've tried to get my head around the perfect word to describe Brendan's story. Rejected maybe? Rejected describes a person who wants to be included but is denied. Guilty perhaps? That's how someone might feel who did something wrong. How about lost? Describes a person on a journey but to where? Lonely is another good one. We have all been there. However, the word that kept coming to me is Empty.

Webster's describes empty as a word meaning without, void or containing nothing. His story began before I made that bet, but I heard about him for the first time in summer of 2014. Roughly six months after the Broncos and I lost in February. I'm not sure why the story came to me, but as I struggled for those four years, his story is where I often found another word that would later describe me. Peace.

Brendan was a team member of the Granite Mountain Hotshots. A group of 20 wildfire fire fighters who travel the country protecting our land, protecting sometimes the unknown, but namely they protect people. They are based out of Prescott, Arizona, not far from my parents' house. I know the area and landscape well. Brendan was recently out of jail, running from a drug addiction, and a host of other issues. He was fatherless and any adult male he hung out with was the wrong man. Without any proper direction in life, he fortunately did find a man named Eric Marsh who turned Brendan's life around. Eric was the superintendent for the hotshot crew who Brendan would eventually work for.

On June 30th, 2013, a wildfire called the Yarnell Hill Fire took the lives of Brendan's entire crew. He was one of 20 men working for the Granite Mountain Hotshots. Brendan, or "Donut" as he was nicknamed, was asked to assist another crew on a watch from a distance where he and his crew were working. The word working is probably an understatement. The wind and fire conditions along with already dry conditions and 100+ degree Arizona heat required a different game plan for fighting that fire. The crew's superintendent Eric knew the land; he also knew how to win battles. He also knew he needed a guy he could trust. He asked Brendan to leave the crew temporarily and go to another point of reference where they could gain some perspective on what the wind was causing the fire to do.

It's a fairly common practice. They do it from the air, other mountain tops, other crews from miles away only need a radio and ground crews across valleys can win the day. The great ones will tell you that figuring out what a fire is doing before it knows what it's doing is a key to winning a battle. Without hesitation, Brendan agreed and was literally off and running.

What nobody knew was how bad the ground conditions were that day. The entire southwestern United States was in real fire trouble. The already dry terrain was baking in the brutal summer heat. The Yarnell fire started from a lightning strike, and was spreading faster than anyone could comprehend. The hotshots from Granite Mountain had come a long way in a short time. They were a new outfit, doing some unusual things with fire containment.

Just a short time before the blaze in Yarnell, the Granite Mountain Hotshots were working a blaze called the Doce Fire just west of Prescott, Arizona. Of all things you hear about a fire crew saving, this was an unusual one. Saving lives, livestock, property, or structures is just in a day's work. They and the other crews working Doce had done their jobs well. Early predictions from various experts were everything in and around the Doce fire was gone or quickly going to be gone. The Granite Mountain team got in front of that issue and started changing some of those predictions.

One item The Granite Mountain crew knew of was something sacred to the people in that area of Arizona. The oldest living Alligator Juniper in the world is located there. Thanks to Eric, Brendan, and the entire Granite Mountain crew, it still stands today. You can find the picture all over the web. Some of the more famous pictures show the tree with the crew from Granite Mountain. That tree would have been gone for sure. The picture is the last of the crew together before they would perish some weeks later. Brendan is in that picture.

On the dreaded day some weeks later, everyone in town had gathered to receive news of what had unfolded earlier. From what I read, I can only imagine what the scene was like that evening. Mothers and fathers, wives and children, and friends from all walks of life were all hearing from the news that 19 out of 20 men from the Granite crew had died. The first crews at the scene reported back that 19 bodies in total had perished. But the crew had 20 team members. Did someone survive? Who survived? As word moved around the community that day about the tragedy that had unfolded, one of the local schools opened its gymnasium as a gathering spot for anyone seeking information or wanting to help. The school is where all the families and friends assembled. For many that day, I'm sure each was just seeking the same thing. Hope.

Hope that the one survivor was dad. Their dad. Maybe for others it was a husband or a boyfriend. Fathers and mothers, brothers and sisters hoping that their son or brother was going to walk through that door. Brendan was on his way, but for 19 families, he was not the man they were hoping for. It was late, only the glow of the surrounding fire and countless emergency lights lit the night. I can't imagine how many prayers were said and negotiations were made with God if only he blessed them with their loved one. As the scene at the school intensified, the crowds grew larger, tears and sobbing intensified. Brendan was just down the street.

Sometime later that same night, Brendan made it through the doors. He was given a ride there by another crew. I can only imagine the anxiety in his head and the hell in his heart. What I fear most was, what was the scene through his eyes? The gymnasium was packed. Some say everyone in town was in that gymnasium. Sadly, nobody was there hoping, praying to see Brendan.

Families were packed together trying to comfort one other. Friends praying, holding out for any kind of hope that the man walking through the doors was this man, or maybe that man. Please be my dad. My brother or my husband, please God, let number 20 be mine. Each group in the gym wasn't rooting against the other families, but they weren't rooting for them either. When Brendan did enter, it was only a second, maybe two, before the entire room collapsed in grief. The man, Brendan, that walked through the doors had to endure the pain, rather hell, of not being the man anyone wanted to see.

Again, I've never met Brendan, but maybe one day if I ever do, I'll ask him how he did it. I'd like to know how he got out of bed the next morning. I'd like to ask many other questions too, but most won't really matter. What would I really like to also ask is if he felt empty?

Speaking from experience, that's a bad place to find yourself. There's a lot of bad thoughts and at times behavior, when you find yourself empty. Most we cause all on our own. Sometimes others cause, but Brendan's? His "cause" wasn't his or anyone's cause, and it was one of the worst.

I've revisited this story a few times during my four years of hell back then. The minute the movie came out, I watched it twice, the same day! I've read a few stories about that fire and that crew a few times. They were that good. At the same time, I've not read some stories and tales to the end as they were that bad. The entire thing breaks my heart, but as I mentioned before, oddly I find peace for myself in Brendan's story.

I lost a few dollars and was harassed by a bookie and his thugs. A few friends went away and at a couple of jobs I had to deal with some thugs making threatening phone calls. I had a family member or two go to bed a bit worried every now and then. That's it though, nothing like what Brendan had and has had to endure.

Brendan's story is an amazing tale of survival. For me it is anyway. Here's a guy who should have never been part of the 20. The 20 men of Granite Mountain Hotshots were some of the best in the world at what they do. They were the elite, and in the beginning of his story, Brendan was far from elite. What odds and what kind of work was required for Brendan to turn it around? For himself, for his family, for his crew of 20?

I think often of the days, weeks, and months following the

tragedy when he could no longer call anyone on his crew. His superintendent Eric would never follow his lead or be able to ask for his advice, on anything. I think of relationships with the family and friends of the other 19 who in that gymnasium looked at him as the last man they wanted to see. I often wonder what advice a guy like that who just went through that hell would give to me after hearing my ordeal.

Of course, by comparison, our struggles were caused by completely different things. Death and debts aren't even in same zip code. I'd never assume my worst day was even close to something like what he had experienced. I'm just always drawn to good stories, and anything dealing with overcoming obstacles I've always gravitated towards. Most would probably agree that wherever you can find joy, comfort or some grace, do it. This story just helped bring some perspective on some important things in life. I was so filled with guilt, losing those priorities while focusing on nonsense. After reading about this event, and watching the movie about his story, there were many mornings when I might be feeling down, depressed or sometimes even mad that I said aloud to myself, "What would Brendan do here?" Oddly, it helped.

# 20

# June 7, 1995

*"Every Father should remember one day his son
will follow his example, not his advice."*
—Charles Kettering

THERE IS A STORY ABOUT AN ALCOHOLIC FATHER who had two sons. One son, now a middle-aged man, just couldn't get it together in life. For some odd reason, problems in both his personal and professional life seemed to follow him around like a bad penny. Relationships just wouldn't last, constant money issues, bad health, legal problems, no friends of any worth, a bad outlook on life, and the list goes on and on. He had served some jail time for repeated DUI's and couldn't hold down a job for any length of time at any time in his life. He was a good guy, but he just struggled from one day to another, year in and year out. He was once asked by a random neighbor, "What happened to you?" Heavy hearted and rather sad to admit he replied, "I had an alcoholic father."

His brother was a complete contrast. He recently celebrated his 25th year married to the same woman, the love of his life. The company that he started in his home with almost no money had grown to several thousand employees some 20 years later. His two kids, both in college, were making plans for highly successful careers of their own. He and his wife had just donated their millionth dollar to charity, a goal they set together in their first year of marriage. Last summer, he competed and almost won a triathlon he was competing in, in his 50s. The same neighbor asked him the same question that he had asked his brother just a few days before, "What happened to you?" Enthusiastically and with a smile he replied, "I had an alcoholic father."

A fun little story that should remind us of all the value of perspective and of what certain events can do to shape your life, both good and bad. All the experiences mentioned in this book are of my own doing. I am responsible for everything good, bad or somewhere in between. People choose to blame someone for their falling short or having "issues." This mess, I did this all on my own. I did, however, see some behaviors that were probably not the best for me at different times in my life. No excuses, and certainly nobody is to blame except me, but I must share some other stories that are 100% true. Each of them probably uniquely had just a tad bit of responsibility, or rather added to the building block on how or why a guy might place a $50,000 wager like I did. I hope you enjoy this short ride, I certainly did.

It was the fall of 1989. I was in my second year of college and as you've read, playing poker or making wild wagers was the norm, day in and day out. Very often for me and a handful of friends, it was all we did. What wasn't the norm was casino-style gambling. That wouldn't come to Colorado until 1991. So, when my grandmother and Mom worked up a quick Thanksgiving weekend drive out to Vegas, they asked if I would like to come. I think my reply was something like "Hell yes, I want to come!" Truth told, the Tuesday before Thanksgiving when we started the journey heading out west, I was the most excited person in the minivan. I spent the majority of the 12-hour drive conspiring how to gamble. I had two minor issues, however.

The first issue, I was only 19. I'd been buying beer in college the last year with the world's worst fake ID, so that little detail wasn't going to stop me from gambling if I could help it. But this would be my first attempt using that ID outside campus. The Vegas staff "might" notice the delaminating and yellow cardboard ID?? It was so bad, it was funny. The second, and oddly larger issue was that I, being in college, was the typical broke student. In my wallet on that drive out were maybe 40 bucks and that terrible ID.

In Vegas, once we arrived it appeared from the onset, my purpose from my parents' perspective was to keep an eye on, almost babysit, my two younger brothers when all the adults were playing. One brother was 16 and the other was 11. That was my parents' plan, not mine. It was less like babysitting and more like managing the kids' bankroll that Mom and Dad kept providing throughout the day. They'd feed me money to keep us entertained in the mezzanine of the Circus Circus casino while they fed money into slot machines down below. If you've ever been to the casino there, you understand. Dad would give me, say 60 bucks, about every hour or so when I dropped in on him on the ground floor for our entertainment upstairs. It was to be split up between the brothers, and as you can imagine, I was supposed to split it up evenly between us. Ten bucks for each of them and the other $40 was for me. Hey, I was building my bankroll before my plans to hit the casino floor later that day.

After just a half day of eating corn dogs and cotton candy upstairs my plan was coming together nicely. I was still "watching" my brothers play toss across and whatever other weird Circus games, and I had already amassed over $100 in my personal gambling funds. For a 19-year-old college kid, that might have been the largest sum of money I had ever amassed at one time. This was actually looking like the easiest job I'd have for years to come. If I could somehow bump into my grandparents downstairs, perhaps I could turn up the "kids donation fund" to the keep-us-kids-away-from-the-adults job I was managing. I think before dinner that first day, I was sitting on around $200. Unreal, the excitement for my first assault on slot machines was coming soon. Oddly, that was more money in my wallet than I had ever had, amassed in a short couple of hours. My casino fund problem had been solved, at least temporarily.

That was Wednesday, day one of our trip. I didn't get an opportunity until the next day to possibly hit the casino on my own. That would be Thanksgiving, and it wasn't spent at Circus Circus. It was, from the start at least, supposed to be a family day. Full of sightseeing and other crap that Grandma and Mom had worked up in their hearts, but nobody else in our crew wanted to do. I went along with it, after all, it was a family vacation on a major holiday. I'm sure you have perhaps been there as well, maybe not in Vegas, but somewhere else with the entire family holding hands, aweing at the surrounding sites while humming something from *The Sound of Music*. Well, that worked until about noon for my grandfather and he put the halt on that BS. Thank God! Gramps came to Vegas to gamble, and little did he or anyone else know, so did his grandson.

At about 1:00 in the afternoon while everyone was separated, (remember this is pre-cell phone days) we tried—tried being the key word—to find a nice restaurant and do the whole Thanksgiving meal thing. That time and place would become the adventure of the weekend and a favorite memory for anyone there for years to come. Seven of us in total, and at no point in three hours could we get everyone in the same space for five minutes to make a lunch decision. Perhaps you can visualize the scene, maybe you've been there yourself? Everyone was distracted, being pulled away for one reason or another, but by 4:00, we hadn't eaten a bite and my grandmother snapped.

We were standing in front of Slots-O-Fun, just next door to Circus Circus and Grandma went inside to the little café / snack stand. They served foot-long hot dogs and shrimp cocktails. The rest of us followed along and all ordered the same. We all added a soft drink, grabbed the first plastic table and chair and all sat down, said grace and had our Thanksgiving meal in the middle of the casino. It was the best. Chili cheese hot dogs and rubbery shrimp cocktails. It was a true Griswold vacation-like adventure. Do I ever wish I had a photo of us enjoying that meal.

After dinner I was able to slip away and hit the El Rancho across the street on my own. My two brothers hit the bed with Mom upstairs and the other adults all went off in their own direction. My first ever slot machine was a video blackjack machine. You had to load quarters in the thing and could adjust your bet between 25 cents and 25 dollars. Damn, that's a lot of quarters. Anyway, I burnt through 40 bucks or so betting a dollar or two in only a few minutes. I should have picked up right there that they don't build these buildings on winners. But wow, the money was going fast.

I moved to some random three-reel Lucky 7 slot machine. Again, more quarters and now my first ID sting. The change lady, a gal walking around with some change cart was probably 108 years old. Did I mention the El Rancho was an older property; building, staff and all? Anyway, I passed that hurdle, and passed another $40 into a machine in record time. I was down $80 but was still pumped to be doing this gambling thing. As bad as I wanted to hit the tables, I couldn't chance it and stuck to the quick bleed of the slots. My luck had to change soon.

This is the part of the story that I would have loved to say I turned things around. Even though I did move around a tad and try a few different machines, it was all the same result. Nothing positive really happened. About 2 hours later, walking across the strip heading back to the room, I was down to only $10 in my wallet. I think the best thing I hit was 15 coins on a mixed bar, and that was once!

The rest of the weekend was more family time, and the opportunity to rebuild my bankroll and eventually gamble never panned out. Two days later, just like that, my first, "real gambling" weekend had ended. We all packed into the family truckster and drove east for what seemed like an eternity. If you have ever made that drive through Utah, you know exactly what I'm talking about. Even though the gambling experience wasn't positive, something about the atmosphere took ahold inside me. Some of you reading this also know what I'm talking about. I knew sometime soon, I'd be back.

That would be less than two years later, my 21st birthday to be exact. Still in college, still playing cards often on campus, Mom called yet again with an invite for another trip to sin city. My grandfather was not a fan of flying and was retired. Translated, this journey would also be by the same minivan, yet again. I didn't care, this was now going to be my first "legal" experience gambling, and I couldn't wait. This time we left my slightly older little brothers home and I brought my college girlfriend along. Six of us packed in the minivan and we headed out for our 12-hour road trip on a Thursday.

We had planned on driving through the night, but around 3 in the morning, my grandmother blew a fuse and demanded we stop in Mesquite, Nevada to rest for the night. It's a small gambling and golf town about an hour and a half outside Vegas. I'll always remember this day as it was a Friday, the morning of my 21st birthday and the day I hit my first slot machine jackpot. It was only a nickel machine, but the story is oddly fun.

I was saving my money (a little larger bankroll than the 40 bucks I brought when I was 19) for the larger casinos in Vegas later that day. However, while waiting for breakfast that morning, my mother and grandmother started playing the nickel machines right by the coffee shop. They were still the hand-load style machines, meaning you pumped coins in and either pressed a spin button or pulled the arm to set the reels spinning. Now my grandmother was using the side of the machines to break open the coin rolls and on one of her attempts, she dislodged some nickels on the floor and left them. I kid you not, she barely eyeballed them and kept walking around pumping slot machines and spinning away.

Well, I immediately went after them on the floor here, there, and everywhere. I think I may have collected 10 or 11 nickels and promptly started stuffing them into machines myself. On the second machine I put coins in, on its first spin; I hit the red, white and blue triple 7 machine jackpot for $580 bucks. Mind you, this was the second machine I ever played legally, and I hit the jackpot on a nickel machine.

Dad was the first to high five me and Gramps was smiling ear to ear about 10 feet away. Mom came in for a quick hug and Grandma, well, she billed me. That's right, billed me. We had a playful argument about the nickels and whose property that was. She proclaimed she was going to gather them up after her roll was gone and I had acted too quickly. As you can imagine, I lost that argument and only collected $280, or half of my first jackpot. I was ok with it, the trip was starting off with a bang, she and I were now both up, and Vegas was yet to come.

That was the highlight of day one of legal gambling. For the next couple of days, just like for most gamblers, Vegas cleaned me out. I tried every version of every table game they offered. I drank as many free cocktails as I could get ahold of. We all had a great time, ate well, played hard, and went to a show; in short, we had a blast for three days. On Sunday's drive home a few days later I chuckled with everyone about the nickel slot machine. Little did I know, nickels would have an odd spot in a future slot machine win.

It was a few years later, 1995 to be exact. I had married, and we already had a son. We were both working a ton, trying to save money to pay bills and buy a home. We were a young couple and working towards bigger and better things in life. Gambling, even occasional cards weren't something I was able to do often if ever at all. That would change in June of that year.

June 7th is a day I'll never forget. My wife and I both, by

accident, had the same day off and it was rather nice outside. Early in the morning we randomly chose to hit a local lake around Denver and take our son fishing. It was shaping up to be a perfect family day. Little did we know how oddly perfect it would turn out.

The lake was full of other families doing the same thing. We were all standing around trying to fish, but it was more like doing nothing and fighting to keep dogs and kids out of the water. To say anyone was fishing that day isn't the correct term. Nobody anywhere was catching anything, and bites were also infrequent if at all. Roughly two hours into our morning, as luck would have it, I had a decent strike and working the pole to land what nobody had seen all morning, a fish!

Random other fathers, granddads or pretty much anyone with a fishing pole started to walk down the beach and glance at the elusive creature I had hooked. The reel-in was awkward as it appeared that perhaps I was only snagged and was dragging in a branch perhaps. It just didn't appear to be a fish. The odd part was how that branch was moving like a fish but, but there was an odd trail and movement in the water for whatever I was reeling in towards the shore. "What the hell?" exclaimed one onlooker as I reeled in two, yes two fish.

My line had a single hook on it baited with salmon eggs. Pretty standard for lake fishing in Colorado. The hook on the end of my line had somehow made its way into the eye of the swivel attached to another random line with its own hook lodged in my fish's mouth. That line had another line going to another hook about three feet away with you guessed it, another fish. Somehow, someway my bait was consumed by my fish, but the hook from my line never touches the fish, rather found the incredible oddity of hooking itself in the eye of that swivel with one hook in its mouth and another line to another fish hooked regular like. It was the craziest thing fishing I had ever seen. Probably 30 guys at that moment came for a closer look and each of us puzzled by what had just happened. In short, I landed two fish, and my hook never touched a single fish's mouth. If you thought that was nutty, hold my beer.

My family, the three of us, left the lake maybe an hour or so later and had a late lunch before my son got his afternoon nap. The wife and I couched up early afternoon for a mid-day movie right before my phone rang. I was expecting a call, but hoping at the same time the phone didn't ring. I had a friend from out of town who was piece-mealing a bachelor party last minute for the groom of a wedding we were all attending the coming weekend. We couldn't really afford it, I didn't really want to go, but he was a good friend, so I had to say OK.

My wife and I agreed I would only spend 40 bucks from our checking account. After hitting the bank, I ran through the house and cars collecting random change for our bachelor party in Black Hawk later that same day. Casinos still had most of their machines set up to take loose coins. I had also grabbed a single dollar bill that my wife had found in the parking lot and washed in her work pants before letting it dry crumpled up atop the dryer. I think with that dollar and a handful of coins, I had maybe $50 total.

We all arrived in Black Hawk around 9 p.m. Many guys were hitting the tables, but my bankroll wouldn't allow for that, and I was set on taking it easy. If I could somehow stretch this out for the evening, I would be a hero. My plan was the nickel slots. I was the only guy playing slots from our group of about 10 guys. After about an hour or so of everyone completely being unloaded of funds and fun, it was decided that we would pack up, drive back down into Denver and hit a couple of strip clubs. That was something I wasn't looking forward to at all.

Being a team player, I sucked it up and began dumping the remaining coins into slot machines to prepare for the change of plans. I had earlier purchased two rolls of nickels to play along with the old ladies and was wandering around the casino trying to find a nickel machine to rid myself of them. I stumbled across a row of Quarter Mania machines with nobody in site anywhere playing in any direction. In one hand I had two rolls of nickels and with my other I reached into my pocket to retrieve that washed up dollar bill my wife had washed that I had grabbed off the dryer. I'm not sure why, but I wanted to get that thing into a machine before ridding myself of these nickels in the other hand. I tried probably a half dozen times to feed that bill into the bill receiver. It didn't go. Repeatedly on the same machine, I tried to get it to take. Every time it spit it back out, I'd try to flatten the bill and then re-load. After maybe the 10th time or so, it finally gave me 4 credits on the machine.

Now Quarter Mania is a 4-reel, two max coin, progressive machine. I had seen them in Vegas before, but now they were in Colorado. Maybe you have heard of Megabucks? The same company owns and operates the themed machines to casinos all over the world. They have huge jackpots, but come on, it's a slot machine, so I wasn't planning on hitting anything of value. I was just trying to unload all the extra coins and that one-dollar bill before heading to the clubs in Denver.

Spin number one, I bet one quarter of the four quarters that I had. On three reels of that first spin, I matched three cherries and won 15 quarters. I would have hit 30 quarters if I would have loaded the machine with the 2-coin max. Regardless, I now had 18 total quarters. Everyone from the bachelor party was packing into the cars outside and I had to get going. I began to mad rush the machine and pumping two quarters in as fast as I could. I didn't want to hold up the party, but again I hit another couple of mixed bars and now had probably 30 or 40 total quarters and couldn't seem to rid myself of all this loose change. For a brief second I contemplated scooping up the quarters and taking them with these two rolls of nickels I was still holding and just leaving. The clock was ticking, and I needed to go. Two coins at a time, I was as fast as possible loading the machine trying to go broke.

I could probably write another book about what happened that night, but this Quarter Mania story is only a piece of this book and my gambling. It's a great story, with lots of plot twists and turns and what happened that night is something most wouldn't believe. I did have my picture in the Denver Post and many who know me know this is all true. I woke up on June 7th, 1995, and went fishing and caught two fish with one hook. Crazy enough event right there alone. Later that same night I placed a single dollar in a quarter slot machine and about 20 spins in, I hit the mega jackpot for $236,632.34. It was six hours later, roughly 3 a.m. before I finally got my check. My shift at work started at 6 a.m., some three hours later, and yes, I made that shift.

Funny, as I write this, I can tell you with no hesitation, I hate slot machines. In the past 10-plus years, I could safely say that I've maybe placed 100 bucks in a slot machine, and that's in total of all machines. What's the point? It's a complete waste of time, and of course money. There is no control to the outcome, and that form of gambling plays zero interest in any gambling that I have or may still do. People have written strategy books on how to play or beat slot machines, and I think those writers and readers have both lost their minds. You cannot beat a machine.

That was advice my dad gave me. I was in a state park telling my parents who were vacationing the tale about the 50-thousand-dollar wager. He said you can't beat a machine, or people who do this for a living. Be it a casino or a bookie. They do this for a living, and most importantly, they don't lose. My parents knew something was up, and they didn't judge me at all, they only wanted their son happy and healthy. I was well into my payment plan with LT and although they offered help, I didn't accept it. As I continued to spill the beans, their eyes grew wider in amazement and their smiles grew larger. Yes, smiles. As I continued to unload the story, the disbelief and shock of it all turned into genuine laughter.

We spoke for several hours that night and it was so satisfying to come clean. It was also the hardest I had laughed with my parents for some time. Specifically with my father. He just about passed out when I told him about the port-a-potties in Miami. We later spoke about responsibility and even though when at times it being ever so hard, doing the right thing would never be wrong.

Romans 8:28 tells us that God will use all things for good for those that love him. Going through this, I couldn't see what any good would come from this nightmare. It was my father who first suggested that I see this through, correctly, honorably and then something positive would happen. I'm still in that journey, but I can tell you this, the number of others that I speak with and bring comfort to using this story, while they deal with their own issues, I'm sure is part of God's plan. I take a little comfort and enjoy stories from others "coming clean" with their journey and I believe we are all a little better in the end.

I'm not there yet, but I'm well on my way.

# 21

# Buy Your Peanuts

*"Gamblers play just as lovers make love and drunkards
drink – blindly and of necessity, under domination
of an irresistible force."*
—Anatole France

A GOOD FRIEND OF MINE named Mary loves the game of craps. It's
the only kind of gambling she does. It's at the craps table where
we met one day many, many years ago and where we still bump
into one another from time to time. I love it when we do. We hop
right into our last conversation like we just dropped it off the
night before. It may be months between seeing each other, but
either by plan or accident when we meet up, the conversation
is genuine. We talk, we laugh, we cheer when we make a point,
but more time than not, we cry and complain when things don't
work out well on the craps table.

Mary (her real name) is in real estate and incredibly
successful here in Colorado. One Sunday morning, we were with
a couple of our other friends, and we were all on the same craps
table, all having zero luck. If it wasn't for the company around
the table, we would have all been long gone as our wallets were
being repeatedly beat up by each and every player going around
the table. On this particular day we were talking about gambling

one liners, and she dropped a couple of real verbal bombs (a kind of quote that both has no meaning and means everything all in one) that have nothing to do with gambling but at the same time, they say a great deal about the silly industry.

Quote one; "You missed the wedding, but you'll stay for the funeral!" How many times in life do we have an opportunity to do something, and we pause? Perhaps we'll look into an investment opportunity or business idea, and we wait until "Later"? Perhaps in Mary's case, it's a real estate deal, and either the buyer or seller waits and loses money? Many of us have been there in one way or another. Well, the same thing happens in gambling every day. In our case, or rather anyone who plays the game of craps, we all hear the horror of just getting to a table when an incredible roll just occurred. We see the laughter, the won chips in the rail, and whether we ask for it or not, we repeatedly hear the story about how great the last shooter was. That was the wedding, and yes, we missed it. What do gamblers do though? We buy-in hoping to catch part of the winning wave or keep the momentum rolling. A winning run, or in this case "roll," never stops a gambler. More times than not, in our effort to catch a winning run, we stay way too long and end up watching our money die off. "You missed the wedding, but you stay the funeral!"

Quote number two; "don't forget your peanuts when the circus comes to town." The circus of course being gambling, and the peanuts? Yes, that would be your money. You can't go play with the circus without paying for the entertainment.

When the Poker boom was just starting to explode across the globe, I went to a "presentation" given by one of the top players (at the time) in the world. The presentation was in south Denver, conveniently close to my home. It was poker so of course I reserved a spot. It wasn't really "given" as I had to pony up like $60 or something to listen to the man ramble on about his background, poker strategy, and the blah, blah, blah about his thoughts on the game and gambling in general. I was less than impressed that night, but I did read a story years later about the same guy that fascinated me.

This professional poker player was a rather large man. The guy was already a tall man in stature, but for a while in his life, you'd notice his weight before anything else. To say he was a large man was an understatement. I'm not sure about the exact date or what his age was at the time, but at one point at an early age, his doctor had asked him to bring his wife and perhaps some other family with him for a follow-up visit the following week.

The story didn't go into the gist of the original visit to the doctor, and it only briefly touched on the follow-up visit with his wife and family. That wasn't the primary purpose for the story. The short version was he was in bad health and the doctor wanted his family to hear what his current condition was and where his health was going. The doctor suggested that at this early age in life he get his affairs in order, because due to his poor health, and even worse his poor attention to his physical needs, he would be dead soon. I can only imagine how tough that would be to hear.

His wife took the news hard and it was she and his sister who took the news seriously. They led a charge to, in essence, save his life. Immediately the two women and others within the family, along with a couple friends, mapped out a plan to get his health in order. Yes, they even hired some other professionals to complete the mix, as this was a plan of action to get on top of this. Nobody waited either, the very next day following that visit, he and his family were at work to get his health in order. The first order of business was of course his diet. It was aggressive and one of their plans was to eliminate red meat from his diet immediately. That lifestyle choice would later turn into a forever choice for him.

This is where the article got interesting. He still played cards and quite often. From what I gathered, even with the poor diagnosis from the doctor, he didn't miss his regular playing schedule. His sister had gotten to many of his friends and managers of card rooms early in his treatment at some of the casinos that he often visited. She implored each person that she contacted in the early days to keep her brother away from junk food, fried items or any red meat while he was playing cards. Believe it or not, many casinos around the world offer an unbelievable menu table-side for your eating and playing pleasure.

Anyway, in a year's time he had lost somewhere like 100 pounds. I wasn't there obviously, but the article went into how hard he tried to right the ship with his health and wellness. He was winning that battle and mentioned that he enjoyed his lifestyle without red meat. There was still more progress to go, but in a simple year he had beyond turned the corner.

Years later, a good acquaintance and a fellow poker player was in the same Las Vegas card room as our "new" man was one day. Down in weight and on top of his new lifestyle, he was ordering lunch from one of the staff members, when the acquaintance overheard the selection and immediately started mouthing off about our guy's lunch selection.

"A salad?" the acquaintance asked in a heckling fashion.

If you knew the acquaintance and his back story, you'd appreciate the fact it wasn't a simple question or statement. I guess it was an intense verbal assault as our guy was deciding upon lunch. Before the server had even left the table, the nagging and teasing from one to another about our guy and his lunch selection, took on a different turn.

"What's the big deal, I like salads and besides, I will never eat red meat ever again," our guy responded.

"I'll tell you what, you order a cheeseburger, and eat it right now, this cash is all yours!"

The acquaintance paused his blabbing, stared across the table briefly, stood up, walked over and sat down a bundle of cash in front of our guy. I'm not sure the exact amount, nor was the article a 100% on the total, but rumor has it between $25,000 and $30,000 dollars. The side bet was officially on. Many players at this level play big in poker and other kinds of bets as well. Our guy just had to order a cheeseburger and eat the entire thing.

He had corrected some much-needed health issues. Without a doubt, his diet was the big thing that got some things under control in his life. It's also known around the poker community that to this day, he still doesn't eat red meat, and it's been years since he had. With the cash in front of him, the server still waiting to take the order, without hesitation and with the eyes from every other player seated around the table were witnessing this debacle unfold.

Our guy handed the menu back to the server and placed his order with a simple request. "I'll have a side salad, and please make sure my cheeseburger is cooked well done!"

********

The story has nothing to do with me directly, but indirectly it explains a lot. Why do guys like me do dumb things with money? To what extent are we willing to go to find the thrill of victory, even though so often the agony of defeat is right around the corner? Poker is but one way of wagering money. Many do multiple other ways as well. I'll tell you from firsthand experience, poker players don't gamble on the poker table. The good ones? Well, they go to work on the poker table. They never "win" money, they earn it!

Many years ago, Tom Cruise and Paul Newman made a movie called *The Color of Money*. If you have seen the movie, no introduction is necessary. For those who haven't, it's about a couple of guys who meet up and start traveling the pool (balls, not water) community across the country in hopes of winning a title and few bucks along the way. The absolute best and most honest line in the movie that applies to so many areas of life is,

"Money won is twice as sweet as money earned!" If you have ever gambled on anything, what a true statement that line is.

Personally, I've lost a small fortune on a variety of bets both on and off the poker table. I haven't won my fortune yet, but it hasn't been from a lack of trying. Remember the little saying, "Don't forget your peanuts when the circus comes to town!" Gambling at times is a complete side show attraction. A big business for some, but silly games for the rest of us. When the circus comes to town, an opportunity to make money on something foolish, a gambler won't forget their peanuts, i.e., don't miss the chance to make money by making a bet. The number of stories out there about some crazy bet that led to something special could fill the pages of another entire book.

Such is the case with this next story I'd like to share with you. The man in the center of this experience was down and out. To some, the ones that knew him, they knew that they were witnessing something amazing unfold. This was nothing short of a Hollywood movie script. I wasn't involved with any of this, but this should be a legendary event. The length some will go to is truly amazing.

Before the poker explosion in the early 2000s, there was a player who over the previous couple months, had run into some bad luck. He was broke, again. It happens to poker players a lot. We often find ourselves between bankrolls. Anyway, the World Series of Poker was coming up and he was short on cash. He was playing in a low-limit game in a famous poker room on the Las Vegas strip. A pal of his noticed the low-limit he was playing and started to razz him about playing with the old ladies and taking their Keno money. Let's call our player, Brain.

It didn't take long for a few other locals and some friends of Brian's to jump in on the fun. I mentioned earlier about the non-stop teasing and good-natured ribbing that takes place on a card table, but if you've rounded for long enough, you know the verbal wars and random jokes about EVERTYHING can be the best part of playing. Nothing is off limits to a card player. I've lost my bankroll on a hand while crying my eyes out laughing while watching a war of insults and jokes about a guy's wife or some random haircut joke at times. I truly love the social part of the game.

Anyway, our player Brain was "getting it" pretty good. He was playing a low-level limit game. Meaning the bets were capped at the lowest level, the buy in was small, and you couldn't go broke in a single hand. In these games, you can play all day for a hundred bucks. Sounds safe doesn't it. The problem was you could play all day and only win a hundred bucks or so. To anyone who has ever played at a higher level, having to step back, rebuild, or begin again is one of the hardest things you can ever do. Placing your ego aside and swallowing your pride to start again has destroyed more players than anything.

During the good-natured fun, at one point in the discussion the talk about the WSOP Main event came up. The $10,000 buy-in annual championship event was weeks away from starting. Winners of this event back then still received a healthy seven figure payday. As a side note, winning this same event today could make you eight to ten million, even more. Well, the story said the conversation in the card room with Brian and the other guys happened on a Wednesday, maybe Thursday, I can't remember. That will be important in a minute.

Aside from the jokes being hurled towards Brian about his bankroll, someone asked him if he was planning on playing in the Main Event. Sheepishly, Brain who knew his current situation better than anyone, replied with a simple and regretful, "Probably not!"

Same group of guys, just a tad bit later, the talk of running had come up in the room. I need to include this as our boy Brian was overweight and out of shape. Apparently, someone joked about Brian running somewhere to make a quick buck or something. Obviously, he was out of shape and hadn't worked out, much less run anywhere, in quite some time. The chatter and running jabs continued and really got rolling when Brian mentioned that he used to run marathons.

Apparently, everyone there, except Brian, about lost it. Good-humored laughter one second and borderline insult bullying the next. Many there didn't know it, they only assumed he hadn't run anywhere anytime lately, and if he did, it was probably to and from the café for a snack, or the ATM for cash. The conversation graduated from a little teasing to a full-on roast. Brian the Iron Man, the Six Million Dollar Man Brian. I'm sure he heard it all.

What not many people knew there was that growing up, Brian was, in fact, a runner. I believe the article even made note that he ran in college. Obviously, life and some different priorities had caught up with him and he hadn't run in many years. He wasn't lying; he did know how to survive on the track.

"For the right price, I could run a marathon tomorrow," Brian threw out there following one of the insults.

Out of nowhere, "You run a marathon this week; I have your $10,000 entry into the Main Event!" one of his good-natured verbal assaulters tossed out.

Right then and there, with nothing more than a handshake and a couple witnesses, the bet was on. The verbal jabs were immediately over. This was now official business, and nobody was going to get involved that wasn't directly involved. One of the many unwritten rules amongst gamblers and poker players. This was for $10,000 that perhaps Brian could turn into millions. He was good enough on the poker table, but he was going to have to get there first. This was shaping up to be a life-changing bet, but the reality that Brian hadn't run anywhere for many years was still going to be a problem.

The terms were simple. He, the bettor and several friendly onlookers were going to meet up on Saturday morning that same week, yes just a few days later. Brian had to run, not walk 104 times around the track. He could waggle, that's a combination of walking and jogging, but he couldn't stop. Each lap on the track was a quarter mile. 104 times around the track and you have 26 miles. Just a tad short of the official 26.2 miles. They gave him the .2.

It was late spring in Las Vegas, and the weather was already dry and unfriendly hot. Saturday, mid-morning was the decided start time. Every guy participating in the teasing just days earlier was there. There were others, too. They weren't there to make fun or have some laughs this time; they were his fans and support group. Another unwritten rule in the poker community is that you root for people to win on and off the poker table. Brian had his money and way into the WSOP Main Event; all he had to do was survive the next several hours.

A "normal" pace for a marathon would probably be four to five hours for most amateurs. The extreme runners can do a marathon in around two hours. Brian finished his that day in over seven. One of the rules was that he could not walk the run, but the waggle was in use often. Following the conclusion of the 26-mile run, Brian's feet were so badly torn up, bruised, blistered and bleeding, that his next stop was the hospital. He spent the night receiving medical care for his feet, they were in that bad of shape.

Less than two weeks later, with his fresh $10,000 earned bet prize, he made his way to the registration booth at the WSOP. He had a great run that year and went on to cash in the Main Event. He didn't win it, but he did have a deep run, and his pay day was a hefty six figure score. The circus came and went, and Brian made out well, because he didn't forget the peanuts!

I think of this story often. This and many alike. I love any story when someone overcomes an obstacle or endures some level of hardship and ultimately, they win. Like most in a similar situation, I too have had the thought, "If I only can do this, or achieve that, or win this amount, I can do (fill in the blank). It far too many times hasn't served its plan, not yet. I had this story in the back of my mind when I confirmed that bet back on Super Bowl Sunday.

# 22

# Have a Nice Day

*"Rule number one in life, bet on yourself."*
—Shawn Sandt

BEFORE IT ESCAPES ME, thank you for reading my story. I hope you enjoyed it, and maybe can do something positive with it. Along this journey, I did manage to make a few good decisions here and there and today, I'm in a great spot. The where, what, and why isn't important, but I did one day realize that I just wasn't enjoying the gambling. I wasn't also foolish and concluded that if you're not enjoying something in life, dump it! That goes for jobs, relationships, what you eat, drink, or in my case, gambling.

This is maybe an odd request, but if I could ask you to do something, can you look around you, right now and identify who is there? I don't care where you are, stop for a second and just answer this simple question. You might be at the office, at school perhaps, maybe your favorite coffee shop, traveling on a bus, or perhaps waiting at the terminal of an airport. Heck, you might be at home with a loved one on the couch sitting next to you with the teenagers upstairs playing video games. Look around you and identify who is there with or around you?

A famous money and business magazine that starts with the letter "F" did a survey in 2021 and it produced some troubling data. Troubling for anyone with a gambling issue or for society perhaps. Just my opinion on the latter. The amount of people gambling online had doubled in that same year, 2021. And it's only the beginning, many in the gambling profession would claim. Various states in the union currently have legislation on the books for their allowance of online gambling and if those laws are to pass (and they are expected to), the number of online gamblers will again double. Add those gamblers to those who currently frequent their local casino, and the numbers are easy to read. No matter where you are, or what you are doing, odds are one-in-four people around you are gambling on a regular basis. In my circle of friends and family, that number is probably +/- 75%.

Part of the article mentioned a study on New York, the state that had recently approved on-line sports betting. Over 650,000 new accounts were opened online with deposits of 150 million dollars. Those numbers were for week one in business. At the time of this writing, 18 states have legal sports betting online. The largest online platform will handle 1.4 billion dollars of action in 2022. Reminder, that's just one of the online platforms. Additionally, the US has almost 1,000 operating casinos in 42 states and for the first time ever, in 2021 the 50-billion-dollar mark was crossed when $53 billion in casino revenues were reported. In perspective, if for one year, not a single dollar was spent gambling, we could as a nation feed every child in every school in America for the next five years.

I wrestle with these figures quite often. These kinds of numbers and others alike are coming out more and more frequently, sometimes daily. The data is out there and in heavy amounts. Years ago, any article about gaming revenues, gaming expansion, or gaming issues in general, I would hardly even notice in my daily routine. Although I was actively a part of it, it didn't interest me, and it's safe to say, I didn't care or want to know the ugly truth. Now, today I read any and all articles about the subject the minute I run across one.

Every time I buy a Lotto ticket, play poker, or join my annual fantasy football league, the numbers, or rather the trouble behind gambling pops-up in my head. Yes, I still gamble here and there, but I do it at an amount that for the first time since my young adult life I can say, doesn't control me. Before the critics reading this voice their opinion, I'll repeat. It's under control and improving daily. I found help in other, meaningful projects, and many other activities.

Most reading this won't know who Herodotus the famous Greek historian was. He's not all that famous, but I ran across a quote from him once that read, "Of all men's miseries the bitterest is this: to know so much and to have control over nothing." I can't tell you how many times that feeling of no control all the while I knew exactly the trouble, or rather the hell I was getting into. The truth is, however, is my problem and possibly the problem for so many others can be found in another famous quote. Mario Andretti, the famous race car driver was once quoted, "If everything seems under control, you're just not going fast enough."

Translated, winning a $10 bet in high school some 30+ years ago was ever so sweet. I still remember the shot, and the ball going in. His name was Steve, he was kind of an A-hole, but he paid me immediately and I bragged the rest of the day. The bet was the action; the trophy was the $10 bill. Can you imagine being on cloud nine over a ten-dollar bet? Seems silly, I know. What's even more silly is to think that same $10 bet today does absolutely zero for my heart rate. Win or lose, most people, including myself don't even care or bother with such a meaningless wager. Why even make a bet for $10, what's the point? I'd rather play a game of Stunt Poker or Lose Your Ass. At least I might have something to laugh at. Mario Andretti would probably tell you the same thing, just from a different perspective. I'm sure the first time he hit the gas pedal, and his car crossed the 100 miles per hour mark was something unreal to experience. A joy hard to explain even though so many have experienced it. I'm sure today; any talk of going 100 miles per hour would probably be nothing more than a boring conversation to him.

Over the past few years, we've all watched the online gambling business explode. If it isn't legal in your state, it will be soon. I've watched from home here in Colorado, but I've also followed the growth in other places in the country. I have also watched the sports book business come to life as well here in Colorado, from its inception, and it has thrived. All the sports books in each casino do well, all of them. There is a shift in "entertainment" happening, and it's been going on for a while, but as of late, it's picking up speed. People aren't going to the movies anymore, and the mall is a dead man walking. Outdoor activities have always been popular. The indoor joints, however? Those are evolving daily, and that evolution can be seen in the sports book and online wagering industry.

One of my new-found passions, if that's the correct phrase, is to understand the problem, not just for myself, but society. I've run across some other amazing stories. Some of these are older than others, but oddly I drew comfort from the fact that I'm not, nor have I ever been alone. You've probably heard the saying, misery loves company.

Netflix did a series on the Chicago Bulls of the NBA a couple years ago. It was a very well done and entertaining documentary. The show focused on the franchise and how they won so many titles in such a few short years. Of course they discussed issues, problems, successes and failures along the way. They also discussed in-depth the players, coaches, ownership and even some fans. It was about their basketball dynasty and of course it was heavily about their all-star and his greatness. The series did go into his problems off the court as well, even though some are labeled as conspiracy theories, most of those surrounded gambling.

Another story that you will recognize is about a guy we've all heard of. Most everyone knows very well what this guy played and what he did. What he was, was baseball's arguably best player, ever. His list of accomplishments on the baseball field is legendary. If you wanted to write about what he accomplished in baseball, well that could take up a book in itself. Only one issue though. In all your research or study on the man, the ending is all the same. The great life of "the greatest baseball player ever" was tarnished or destroyed by gambling.

I'm still trying not to include names, but in recent years some major news came out about another sport with several of its stars all struggling with gambling. R&A Sports and Marketing did a worldwide survey, and it was estimated that almost 70 million people around the world play golf on a regular basis. It's safe to say, we the people everywhere love golf. If you took the top 25 golfers or so of all time, the number of titles won collectively would be a staggering list. What might be less impressive, or more so depending how you look at it, would be if we counted the amount of money lost through gambling from guys on that same list. I've done the research, and the numbers are mind boggling. Although the data out there isn't 100% scientific, rumors and various other facts point to a troubling number. Of that list of the top 25 players, it's estimated they account in total for several hundred million dollars in money lost through gambling.

What exactly did all this do for me? The blurbs of hardships and numbers I just mentioned above? For many reading this, perhaps not very much, but for me, it was everything. It drew my attention to some issues I needed to deal with. I was forced by my own actions to take a real look in the mirror and come to some hard conclusions. Did I like who I was, what I was doing? Not close, not even by a mile.

I woke up one morning in the middle of my mess devastated by a relationship break-up that I was in the middle of. It was two days prior to Christmas, I hadn't bought a single gift for anyone, and I was completely broke at the same time. I was out of shape, eating poorly, not sleeping and hated my job. Nothing was working, and a friend made a stunning observation. He had just mentioned something in passing, but it stung to hear. He had noticed that I hadn't laughed in months. He was correct, I was absolutely miserable. That day, driving aimlessly around Denver, I knew of two phone numbers that most people have at least heard of. The 1-800 numbers for Gamblers Anonymous and the Suicide Prevention hot line. I called one of them right then and there.

I paid off LT in July of 2018. In total it was just a tad over $65,000 in a little over four years' time. As I mentioned earlier, it was the toughest four years of my life. That last payment, it was pretty easy though. Why? Well, the great Bible verse from the book of Proverbs 27:17 says, "Iron sharpens iron." For me, that translates to being tough or having to endure means that things or people had to be tough on me to get me where I need to be today. I spend more time speaking to people about the dangers of sports betting, and in general "control," which I often in the past have had very little of and at times, none. The great Pythagoras once said, "No man is free who cannot control himself." That's a 100% fact. Not just with gambling, but with many other things in our lives.

Many years after that bet, while writing this, I can tell you that I have not made a single sports bet. Never one time, not a single dollar. Even with all the online access and ease to do so, it's no longer something that interests me. I've been in casinos here and there over the past couple of years and the thought of hitting the sports book does nothing for me. I've had many opportunities and each time I've found that "iron strength" to just say no. I have a different purpose and oddly it was gifted to me from good ole LT. I was reminded one random day and think of this often, that in life, not all setbacks are bad, and almost never final. In chess you must at times move backwards to advance, and in poker, being last is better than being second.

As I mentioned, my final payment to LT was in July. I had a few extra bucks mounting from some work commissions and I paid him with my first check that month. In many previous months, I always paid him at the end of the month. That last payment though was different. It was still a business call just like the previous months. Most of the previous months, I sent a text asking for what bank, what name and what account number. Most months after I acknowledged making the payment, I didn't even get a message back with a thank you. He wanted it to be business, so be it.

The final payment I think may have surprised him; in that I was paying him so early in the month. There was no warm voice on the other end when he said hello. It was just more of the same, just as in the past. Bank name, account holder's name and account number. That was it. I'm guessing at the time he didn't realize that when I had called, I was arranging my last payment. I didn't remind him, but I knew he would know if not then, soon enough. I didn't hear another word from him until September. Some two months later he made an unexpected call.

"I must say, I miss you dude." It was a pleasant tone in his voice, kinda giddy with laughter.

Even though the call caught me off guard, I knew the minute I heard his voice, I knew who it was. I replied also with a kind of pleasant giddiness, "Well I haven't missed you!" We both laughed.

He continued, as always with this guy, it was straight to business. "We have some great promos for our best players.

171

Any action you want on this weekend's games, I'll match your deposit 100%!"

The pause before my reply was almost eerie; it was probably for only a second or two, but it was notably long. Holding the phone to my ear, it weighed heavy, and the pause seemed to go on forever. My mind tipped very slightly on the idea of free money. A thousand dollars bet could net an extra $1,000 profit. Perhaps a $2,500 bet could win $5,000, how sweet that would be? I knew the game (football) well and this weekend had some great matchups. I still watch and can find the "locks" here and there. I did have one ready in my mind when he called that afternoon. As much as I didn't want him to call, I needed him to. Why, you ask?

In as simple and clearly as I could speak, I did finally reply to his offer. After I replied, I merely hung up and blocked the number, forever. I've never had any contact with him again. I came across friendly, after all, why be rude? I really wished LT knew what my reply to his offer really meant. Before hanging up, "LT," I said, "have a nice day!"

From the Author......


THAT PHOTO, NOTHING BUT GREAT LAUGHS and even better adventures that entire weekend. Thanks to each of you who were there. The Broncos may not have done their part, but you all did. Speaking of doing their part, Nancy, this book project would not happen without your countless hours and efforts in so many ways. Thanking you in a few short words is impossible. I cannot express my gratitude, appreciation and love enough for giving me your all.

My dad asked one day about three years in on my adventure what the hell was going on. Fathers always know when something isn't right. I sat with him and my mother telling them the tale you just read and after he picked his jaw up off the floor, he advised me to do two things. Make good on my commitments and write this book. I've done both. Unfortunately, I lost my father before this book was complete. He loved my first book; I know he would have loved this one too. I miss you Dad.

I hope you, the reader, found some joy in my adventure. That's what I'll call it for the rest of my life. I still play fantasy football with some great friends, and we do it for low stakes and I find joy in some guy across the country losing his mind over some random NFL kicker missing a chip shot field goal that cost his fantasy team a win. Many times, that is way better than winning a few bucks. I'm not sure why, but someone else's misery over something they cannot control always makes me laugh.

What doesn't make me laugh is hearing about anyone that is struggling with anything out there. Booze, drugs, violence, or if you are like me, gambling. I know how it feels. It's shameful, it's embarrassing, it hurts, it sucks! But I'm living proof that there's help out there. I'd rather listen to hours of your boring-ass story than hear one nice thing at your funeral. The National Suicide & Crisis Lifeline is simply dialing 988 from any phone. It's private, free and easy. The National Problem Gambling Hotline is 1-800-GAMBLER. The toughest person in the room is one who acknowledges they have a problem, and they act on it.

Thanks to all of you.

Shawn

www.ingramcontent.com/pod-product-compliance
Lightning Source LLC
Chambersburg PA
CBHW030254130626
46549CB00002B/527